The Complete Mueller Pressure Cooker Cookbook

250 Simple & Delicious Recipes For Mueller Pressure Cooker

James Norwood

Warning-Disclaimer

The purpose of this book is to educate and entertain. The author or publisher does not guarantee that anyone following the techniques, suggestions, tInstant Pots, ideas, or strategies will become successful. The author and publisher shall have neither liability or responsibility to anyone with respect to any loss or damage caused, or alleged to be caused, directly or indirectly by the information contained in this book.

Table of Contents

Introduction 11

Breakfast Recipes 15

    Blackberry Oatmeal 15

    Oatmeal Pancakes 15

    Spanish Zucchini Tortilla 16

    Cranberry Oatmeal 16

    Mushroom Eggs Recipe 16

    Ham Mixed Bacon Treat 17

    Delicious Oat Mix 17

    Tomato and Cheese Mix Breakfast 18

    French Toast with Cranberries Recipe 18

    Spinach Mixed Eggs Recipe 19

    Oats with Chia Seeds 19

    Quinoa Vanilla Recipe 19

    Eggs with Cheese and Bacon 20

    Dates Granola 20

    Strawberry and Mango Crunch 21

    Lava Chocolate 21

    Bowl Egg 22

    Hot Scrambled Egg 22

    Peanut Slabs 22

    Blueberries and Cream with Oats 23

    Scotch Rolls 23

    Cut Oats Breakfast 24

    Ginger Quiche 25

    Benedict Asparagus with Eggs 25

    Coconut Yogurt with Blueberries 26

    Raspberry and Oatmeal Pudding 26

Lunch Recipes 27

    Mushroom Mix Recipe 27

    Halibut Fillets 27

    Salmon with Soy Sauce 27

Simple Salmon Cooked Recipe 28

Simply Cooked Shrimp 28

Delicious Crab Meat Recipe 29

Tilapia Delight 29

Sweet Potato with Cheese 29

Spinach Mix Tomatoes 30

Black Beans with Lentils and Veggies 30

Black Beans Chicken Mix 30

Black-Eyed Peas 31

Rice Mixed Beans 31

Borlotti Beans with Tomato Sauce 32

White Beans Recipe 32

Black Beans with Tomatoes 32

Beans with Chickpeas 33

Cheesy Macaroni 33

Lemony Chicken Pasta 33

Lamb with Thyme 34

Lamb Loin Dish 34

Roasted Turkey 34

Cellini Beans with Baby Broccoli and Carrots 35

Broccoli Pasta 35

Hot Red Beans Curry 36

Black Lentils 36

Spinach Orzo 37

Chili Garlic Eggplant Pasta 37

Cottage Cabbage Macaroni 38

Slow Cooked Spiced Cabbage 38

Snacks and Appetizers **39**

Potatoes and Black Beans 39

Sweet Potatoes with Cheese 39

Simple Rice Recipe 40

Rice with Saffron 40

Ripe Plantain Cheesy Patty 40

Ritz Shrimp Snack 41

Avocado Paste Snack 41

Delicious Chorizo Snack 42

Tomatoes Mix Recipe...42

Sweet Potatoes with Butter and Vanilla 43

Quinoa with Vegetables..43

Potatoes with Parsley...43

Cauliflower Onion Mix Recipe 44

Simple Potato Recipe...44

Simple Fries...45

Coated Mozzarella Sticks 45

Mushrooms and Pepper Mix 45

Sweet Potato Wedges 46

Potato Chips..46

Greek-style fried Shrimp...47

Stir Fried Cherry Tomatoes 47

Potato Wings 47

Crispy Okra 48

Crispy Chicken Fritters 48

Spiced Fried Cauliflower 48

Creamy Mashed Potatoes..49

Chickpea Hummus..49

Chicken Bites 50

Ginger Zest Pineapple Slices 50

Vegetable and Eggs..**51**

Spinach and Potato Risotto 51

Zucchini Chips 51

Garlicky Roasted Potatoes 51

Cauliflower Carrot Risotto 52

Pressure cooker Creamy Mushrooms 52

Black Lentils Tacos 53

Stir Fried Garlic Zest Spinach 53

Sweet Potato Casserole 53

Creamy Spinach Pulverize 54

Hot Stir-Fried Chili Pepper...54

Creamy Mashed Potatoes Simmer 55

Fried Potatoes 55

Stir Fried Garlic Mushroom 55

Spiced Zucchini Fingers..56

Thyme Zest Potato Mash..56

Asparagus Chowder...56

Slow-Cooked Cabbage...57

Eggplant and Tomato Curry..57

Chili and Garlic Zest Pumpkin..58

Peas and Carrots with Potatoes 58

Slow Cooked Honey Glazed Carrots......................................58

Tropic Cauliflower Manchurian 59

Garlic Fried Mushrooms..59

Rice with Carrots..60

Tropic Potato Gravy...60

Ground Beef Zucchini Zoodles 61

Spinach Black Beans Chili...61

 Sweet Potato Mash with Oregano 61

Mashed Potato Pilaf...62

Eggplant and Potato Gravy 62

Cabbage with Potatoes 63

Cheese Omelette...63

Egg Scramble..64

Egg and Onion Frittata..64

Egg and Carrots Crumb 64

Half Fry Eggs 65

Bell Pepper and Egg Tortilla..65

Hard Boiled Eggs 65

Avocado eggs 66

Roasted Eggs Gravy 66

Squash with Eggs 66

Pepper Egg..67

Tomato Eggs 67

Zucchini Egg 67

Egg Mac...68

Poached Eggs 68

Coated Eggs..68

Spinach Egg Frittata 69

Asian Style Steamed Eggs 69

Eggs Steamed in Avocado 70

Soups and Stews..**71**

    Pumpkin and Potato Soup 71

    Mushroom Soup 71

    Cauliflower Soup 72

    Peas and Spinach Soup 72

    Shrimp Soup 73

    Chicken Corn Soup 73

    Chickpea and Basil Soup 73

    Chicken and Mushroom Soup 74

    Turkey Mixed Soup Recipe 74

    Cheesy Chicken Recipe 74

    Chicken and Green Onion Soup 75

    Vegetable Broth with Veggies Soup 75

    Black Beans Mix Soup 75

    Corn and Potato Mix Soup 76

    Delicious Full Chicken Soup 77

    Chicken Noodle Soup.. 77

    Beef Soup 77

    Sweet Potato Soup 78

    Vegetable Soup 78

    Garlic Chicken and Egg Soup 79

    Pumpkin Purée Soup 79

    Spinach Soup 80

    Onion and Carrot Soup 80

    Yellow Lentils Hot Soup 80

    Red Beans Soup... 81

    Potato Cream Soup 81

    Butter Squash Soup 82

    Cream of Asparagus Soup.. 82

    Beef and Broccoli Stew 83

    Ginger and Sesame Asparagus Stew 83

    Broccoli and Fenugreek Stew 84

Chicken Recipes..**85**

    Chicken Wings 85

    Hot Chicken Fingers.. 85

Whole Chicken...86
Chicken Nuggets 86
Chicken Pepper Noodles 87
Broccoli Chicken 87
Simple Chicken Wings..87
Delicious Chicken..88
Ground Chicken...88
Chicken Breast with Green Onions 89
Chicken Egg Noodles 89
Chicken Shallot..90
Chicken and Beans...90
Chicken with Sesame oil...90
Chicken Breasts Recipe with Black Beans..............................91
Boneless Chicken with Peanut Butter 91
Chicken Mushroom Mix..92
Chicken Tenders with Garlic..92
Creamy Chicken Noodles 93
Hot Chicken Chili 93
Hot Garlic Chicken Breasts 93
Chicken and Lentil Meal 94
Chicken Mince and Peas 94
Chicken with Avocado Cream 95
Chicken with Sweet Potatoes..95
Asian Style Chicken 96
Chicken with Ginger and Broccolini......................................96

Red Meat...**98**
Pork Steaks 98
Mutton Gravy 98
Ground Meat Lemonade 98
Beef with Peas 99
Diced Meat with Potatoes...99
Simple Meatballs Recipe 100
Sweet Potatoes with Meat...100
Diced Meat with Onions 101
Meat with Peppers..101
Hot Shredded Pork 101

Pork Chops Gravy 102

Beef Okra 102

Slow Cooked Zucchini and Pork 103

Beefalo Wings 103

Pressure cooker Beef Rice 103

Hot and Spicy Beef Gravy 104

Red Beans Tendered Beef 104

Meat Pops 105

Pulled Beef 105

Roasted Bell Pepper with Beef 105

Beef and Peas Gravy 106

Beef and Chickpea Stew 106

Carrot and Beef Stew 107

Fried Okra with Beef 107

Beef Meat with Shallots 108

Sprouts with Pork Portions 108

Lamb with Pomegranate Seeds 109

Ground Beef with Flax Seeds 109

Veal Meat with Asparagus and Almonds 110

Seafood and Fish **111**

Lemon Fish Steaks 111

Creamy Tilapia 111

Roasted Fish with Vegetables 111

Creamy Tuna with Macaroni 112

Fried Tuna with Tamarind Sauce 112

Crispy Crumb Fish 112

Fish Patties 113

Salmon Bowl 113

Tarragon Steamed Fish 114

Fish Smash 114

Coconut Fish 114

Glazed Salmon 115

Teriyaki Salmon with Ginger 115

Desserts 116

Chocolate Pudding 116

Lemon Cake 116

Chocolate Crackers 117

Pumpkin and Pineapple Cobbler... 117

Chocolate Silk Bowls 117

Pineapple and Mango Blossom 118

Mouth-melting Bread Pudding.. 118

Pistachio Cake... 118

Banana and Strawberry Pudding 119

Buttercream Dessert.. 119

Puff Pastry 119

Chocolate Mix Recipe... 120

Honey Pistachio Cake Recipe 120

Carrot and Honey Pie 121

Cherry Delight... 121

Conclusion 122

Introduction

Mueller pressure cooker is a trend in the market for a new style of cooking. It makes your life more more convenient and easier. People usually do not have enough time to cook nowadays, which is why they prefer quick cooking, and here is where the help of mueller pressure cooker comes in! It helps you make food in just a few minutes, without putting in extra effort. Anyone who cooks with an mueller pressure cooker will surely not get tired!

We all love food, and if you haven't bought an mueller pressure cooker, then it is time to get one now. *550 Recipes for Quick, Easy and Delicious Meals* will help you learn how to make all the amazing dishes, whenever you wish to eat them.

Try the amazing recipes of mueller pressure cooker under various sections such as breakfast, lunch, side dishes, snacks, chicken, and desserts.

If you are looking for a proper guide for every kind of food that you can cook in mueller pressure cooker, you should have these recipes in your collection. All the recipes are easy to make with the simple ingredients found in your kitchen all the time. Pick the best recipes you like and start cooking with Mueller pressure cooker now. You will be amazed at how simple it is to use. The machine plays with you, but you need to make sure to handle it with care. It gives you healthy food with all the nutrients your body requires. You can cook a week's food and keep it stored in your fridge with the help of this machine.

There are many features included in the mueller pressure cooker which you can use to make quick dishes. You can set the manual timer along with automatic. It has an automatic timer installed for each recipe's main ingredient, so if you are trying to make something out of chicken, you simply have to press the button which has "chicken" written on it. Once you press it, the timer will be set accordingly, and you will be notified that the dish is ready when the pot beeps. You do not have to stand in the kitchen, waiting for the recipe to cook – you can do other things while the food gets ready for you!

Mueller pressure cooker makes life easier by giving quick results to its users. Any recipe can be cooked in the mueller pressure cooker. If you do not have enough time in the morning, then all you need is a quick recipe for breakfast with the mueller pressure cooker. Learn the recipes now, so you do not have an empty stomach when you leave for work or school.

You can cook in mueller pressure cooker the whole day and you still won't be able to get enough of this awesome innovation. It is designed beautifully and creates less hassle for people who do not have enough time to cook.

The recipes are short and easy to understand. Anyone can make the recipes with the mueller pressure cooker. You just need to know the right measurements, and you will have a great recipe ready for you. You do not have to deal with fire or flames on the stoves; mueller pressure cooker has made life easier for the people now. Once you know how to cook with mueller pressure cooker, you will want to cook with it every time. There are a variety of recipes found in this book to try, so get started now, without wasting any time!

Once you get your hands on mueller pressure cooker, you will be so pleased that you will want to cook every dish in this pot. This is an amazing product for working people who cannot take the time to cook food. If you are worried that the taste will change if you cook in this pot, do not be concerned about that. You simply have to add all the ingredients in the pot and it will give you great results within few minutes.

Why Mueller Pressure Cooker?

It has a variety of single-key operation buttons to help you cook the most common foods in the easiest way.

These Preset Programs are:

Meat, Poultry, Vegetable, Steam, Risotto, Oatmeal, White Rice, Canning, Beans, Broth, Yogurt, Soup, Multigrain, Sterilize, Chili, Cake, Sauté, Egg, Keep Warm

COOK 2 MEALS SIMULTANEOUSLY

Buying a Mueller Pressure Cooker gives you another advantage and that's the additional steel rack that comes in the package, and which makes possible to cook 2 meals at the same time. Really efficient and time-saving!

Tips to use the Pressure cooker

Always follow the specific directions and cautions provided by the manufacturer for using Mueller pressure cooker.
Do not fill the pressure cooker more than 2/3 full (or more than 1/2 full when cooking soups and stews).
Try to cook recipes with six or fewer ingredients.

General Time Chart for Cooking Foods

RED MEATS		
Round Steak	1/4-inch-thick	4 minutes
Beef Stew	cubed	20 minutes
Ribs		4 minutes
Lamb Chops	1/4-inch-thick	3 minutes
Leg of Lamb	3 pounds	40 minutes
Pork Chops	1/7-inch-thick	5 minutes
Pork Steak	1/4-inch-thick	3 minutes
Veal Roast	3 pounds	45 minutes
POULTRY		
Whole Chicken	3 to 5 pounds	30 minutes
Boneless chicken parts	cut into pieces	3 minutes
Boneless half breast		6 to 7 minutes
Chicken Legs		8 minutes
Chicken Thighs		6 to 8 minutes
Boneless thighs or breasts, frozen		6 to 8 minutes
Ground chicken	1 pound	2 to 4 minutes
Turkey, cut into pieces		2 to 4 minutes
Turkey, boneless	1/2 breast	18 to 20 minutes
SEAFOOD		
Clams		3 minutes
Crab Legs		2 minutes
Whole fish		4 to 5 minutes per 1/2 pound
Scallops		1 to 2 minutes
Shrimp	medium	2 minutes

FROZEN VEGETABLES		
Asparagus		2 minutes
Beans		2 to 3 minutes
Broccoli		2 to 4 minutes
Brussel Sprouts		2 to 4 minutes
Cauliflower		2 to 3 minutes
Corn on the cob		3 minutes
Corn, kernels		2 minute
Mixed vegetables		3 minutes
Peas		2 minute
FREASH VEGETABLES		
Artichoke	whole	10 to 12 minutes
Asparagus	spears	12 to 14 minutes
Beans		2 to 3 minutes
Broccoli		2 to 3 minutes
Carrots		4 to 5 minutes
Cauliflower		5 to 7 minutes
Greens		2 to 3 minutes
Onions		7 to 10 minutes
Potatoes	whole	13 to 16 minutes
Potatoes Sweet	whole	9 to 10 minutes
Pumpkins	wedges	9 to 11 minutes
Squash, acorn	halves	7 to 8 minutes
Tomatoes	whole	3 to 4 minutes

Breakfast Recipes

Blackberry Oatmeal

(Time: 45 minutes \ Servings: 2)

INGREDIENTS:

1 cup oats chia seed
1 cup blackberries
1 cup cream milk

¼ cup caster sugar stevia
4 tablespoons honey
2 tablespoons butter, melted

DIRECTIONS:

- Combine the oats, cream milk, sugar and butter in a bowl.
- Transfer the oats mixture to the Mueller pressure cooker and place the blackberries on top, cover with a lid.
- Cook on OATMEAL mode for 10 minutes.
- Drizzle honey on top.

Oatmeal Pancakes

(Time: 25 minutes \ Servings: 4)

INGREDIENTS:

1 cup oats chia seed
1 cup almond flour
½ cup caster sugar stevia
¼ teaspoon baking soda
½ teaspoon baking powder
2 eggs

1 cup milk
2 tablespoons sour cream
1 pinch salt
4 tablespoons butter
strawberries for garnishing

DIRECTIONS:

- Sift flour, sugar, baking powder, baking soda, salt and set aside.
- Beat the eggs for a minute and add in milk, and sour cream, mix well.
- Add the sifted flour mixture and oats, mix thoroughly with a spatula.
- Melt butter in the Pressure cooker on SAUTÉ mode.
- Ladle the butter in the pot and spread in a form of cake.
- Cook for 2-3 minutes on one side, then flip and cook until brown.
- Transfer to a serving platter and drizzle honey.
- Top with strawberries before serving.

Spanish Zucchini Tortilla

(Time: 15 minutes \ Servings: 3)

INGREDIENTS:

3 eggs
1 large zucchini
1 onion, chopped
½ teaspoon thyme, chopped

¼ teaspoon salt
¼ teaspoon white pepper
2 tablespoons olive oil

DIRECTIONS:

- Cut the zucchini into thin strips and set aside.
- Crack the eggs in a medium bowl and whisk for 1 minute.
- Add the zucchini strips, onion, thyme, salt, and pepper, mix well.
- Add 3-4 cups of water into the Pressure cooker and place a trivet or stand inside it. Now spray a medium-sized baking dish with olive oil, transfer the eggs mixture into a pan and place on a trivet.
- Cover the pot and cook on EGG mode for 10 minutes.

Cranberry Oatmeal

(Time: 40 minutes \ Servings: 5)

INGREDIENTS:

2 cups oats
2 cups milk
1 egg, whisked
1 cup cranberry sauce
½ cup brown sugar

2 tablespoons honey
½ teaspoon ginger powder
1 pinch salt
4 tablespoons butter, melted
2 tablespoons olive oil

DIRECTIONS:

- Grease the Pressure cooker with olive oil.
- Combine the oats, milk, egg, butter, cranberry sauce, honey, brown sugar, ginger powder, and salt in a bowl.
- Transfer to the greased Pressure cooker and cover with a lid. Cook on SLOW COOK mode for 40 minutes.

Mushroom Eggs Recipe

(Time: 15 minutes \ Servings: 3)

INGREDIENTS:

1 cup mushrooms, sliced
4 eggs
2 tomatoes, chopped

1 cup basil, chopped
1 tbsp. butter
salt and pepper, to taste

DIRECTIONS:

- Whisk eggs in a bowl.
- Add salt and pepper, tomatoes, basil and mushrooms.
- Mix well.
- Grease a round baking tray and pour the mixture into it.
- Place it in the pressure cooker and cook for 10 minutes on EGG setting.
- When done, enjoy the delicious mushroom treat!

Ham Mixed Bacon Treat

(Time: 19 minutes \ Servings: 4)

INGREDIENTS:

4 eggs
1 cup milk
3 slices bacon
1 lb. ground sausage

1 cup ham, diced
3 green onions, chopped
2 cups cheddar cheese
salt to taste

DIRECTIONS:

- Whisk eggs with milk in a bowl.
- Add salt to mixture and then pour it into the pressure cooker.
- Mix bacon, ham and sausage in the pot.
- Sprinkle with green onions and cover it all with cheddar cheese.
- Let it cook for 15 minutes on MANUAL mode.
- When ready, take it out and serve!

Delicious Oat Mix

(Time: 15 minutes \ Servings: 4)

INGREDIENTS:

1 tbsp. butter
2 cups oats chia seed
1 cup almond milk
2 cups shredded coconut

1 cup dark chocolate chips
½ cup sliced almonds
salt to taste

DIRECTIONS:

- Sauté the butter in the pressure cooker.
- Add almond milk, oats, salt and chocolate chips.
- Cook it on OATMEAL setting for 10 minutes.
- When ready, take it out and sprinkle with shredded coconut and sliced almonds.

Tomato and Cheese Mix Breakfast

(Time: 15 minutes \ Servings: 3)

INGREDIENTS:

4 slices bread
1 cup spinach, chopped
½ cup cheese, shredded

1 tomato, chopped
salt and pepper, to taste

DIRECTIONS:

- Place the bread as a layer into a round baking tray.
- Add spinach, tomato and cheese.
- Sprinkle with salt and pepper.
- Cook in the pressure cooker for 10 minutes on MANUAL mode.

French Toast with Cranberries Recipe

(Time: 15 minutes \ Servings: 4)

INGREDIENTS:

2 ½ cups cranberries
½ cup orange juice tea
½ cup sugar stevia

½ tsp. cinnamon powder
salt to taste

FRENCH TOAST

3 tbsp. butter
½ cup sugar stevia
2 ½ cups whole milk
2 eggs

2 orange zest
½ tsp. vanilla extract
½ loaf of bread, cubed

DIRECTIONS:

- Put orange juice, sugar, cinnamon powder, salt and cranberries in the pressure cooker.
- Cook on MANUAL mode for 10 minutes.
- When done, put in a container and keep it aside.
- Whisk eggs and butter in a bowl. Add sugar. Whisk well.
- Now add milk, orange zest and vanilla extract.
- Meanwhile, place the layer of bread in the pressure cooker.
- Pour the mixture over it.
- Cover the lid and let it cook on BEANS mode for 20 minutes.
- When ready, serve with the sauce that you made in step 1.

Spinach Mixed Eggs Recipe

(Time: 14 minutes \ Servings: 3)

INGREDIENTS:

6 eggs
1 cup milk
2 cups baby spinach, chopped
½ cup seeded tomato

2 green onions, chopped
2 cups cheddar cheese
salt and pepper, to taste

DIRECTIONS:

- Mix eggs with milk in a bowl.
- Put it into the pressure cooker.
- Add salt and pepper, seeded tomato, baby spinach, green onion and cheddar cheese.
- Cover with the lid and let it cook on EGG mode for 10 minutes.
- When done, serve and enjoy!

Oats with Chia Seeds

(Time: 15 minutes \ Servings: 2)

INGREDIENTS:

1 tbsp. butter
½ cup oats
2 cups water
½ cup cream

½ cup chia seeds
1 cup strawberries, sliced
2 tbsp. brown sugar
salt to taste

DIRECTIONS:

- Put butter into the pressure cooker and select the sauté option.
- When the butter melts, add oats, cream, water, chia seeds, brown sugar and salt.
- Mix well.
- Let it cook on OATMEAL mode for 10 minutes.
- When it beeps, take it out and serve with the strawberry slices on top.

Quinoa Vanilla Recipe

(Time: 15 minutes \ Servings: 3)

INGREDIENTS:

1 cup uncooked quinoa
2 cups water
2 tbsp. Maple syrup

1 tsp. vanilla
2 tbsp. cinnamon powder
a pinch of salt

TOPPINGS:

fresh berries, cherries, crushed almonds

DIRECTIONS:

- Mix water, maple syrup, quinoa, vanilla, salt and cinnamon in the pressure cooker.
- Set the pressure to 5 minutes on MANUAL setting..
- When the sound beeps, turn it off and let it rest for 10 minutes.
- Release the pressure and then open the pot.
- Remove the quinoa from the bowl and dress it with any of your favorite toppings mentioned above.

Eggs with Cheese and Bacon

(Time: 14 minutes \ Servings: 4)

INGREDIENTS:

5 eggs
½ tsp. lemon pepper seasoning
3 tbsp. cheddar cheese, grated

2 green onions, chopped
3 slices bacon, crumbled

DIRECTIONS:

- Whisk the eggs in a bowl and put them in the pressure cooker.
- Now mix the cheddar cheese, green onion and bacon with the eggs.
- Let it cook for 10 minutes on high pressure on MANUAL mode.
- When done, season it with lemon pepper and enjoy!

Dates Granola

(Time: 35 minutes \ Servings: 2)

INGREDIENTS:

2 cups granola
1 cup dates, seeded, halved
1 cup milk
¼ cup peanuts
½ cup coconut milk

¼ cup coconut flakes
1 egg, whisked
¼ cup brown sugar
1 pinch salt
2 tablespoons butter, melted

DIRECTIONS:

- In a bowl, add the dates and the milk and mash using a fork until smooth.
- Now add the brown sugar, granola, salt, butter, peanuts, and egg, and mix very well.
- Transfer to a greased Mueller pressure cooker and cook for 35 minutes on SLOW COOK mode.

Strawberry and Mango Crunch

(Time: 35 minutes \ Servings: 5)

INGREDIENTS:

2 cups strawberries, sliced
2 cups mango, chunks
1 cup mango juice
1 package biscuits, crumbled
½ cup all-purpose flour

1 cup milk
1 egg, whisked
¼ cup caster sugar
4 tablespoons butter, melted

DIRECTIONS:

- In a bowl, add all-purpose flour, biscuits, egg, sugar, mango juice, and milk and mix well.
- Spread into a greased baking dish and press using a spoon.
- Now drizzle butter and top.
- Add the mango chunks and the strawberries.
- Place a trivet into the Mueller pressure cooker and add 3-4 cups of water.
- Put a baking dish on a trivet and cover the pot with a lid.
- Cook on MANUAL mode for 20 minutes.

Lava Chocolate

(Time: 30 minutes \ Servings: 3)

INGREDIENTS:

1 cup raw chocolate, crumbled
½ cup cocoa powder
½ cup all-purpose flour
1 cup cream milk

1 egg, whisked
¼ cup caster sugar
4 tablespoons butter, melted
1 cup cream, whipped

DIRECTIONS:

- In a bowl, add the all-purpose flour, egg, cocoa powder, chocolate, sugar, butter, and milk, beat with a beater for 1-2 minutes.
- Transfer this mixture into the Mueller pressure cooker and cook on CAKE mode for 30 minutes.
- Now transfer to a serving dish and top with whipped cream.
- Sprinkle with chocolate flakes.
- Serve and enjoy.

Bowl Egg

(Time: 15 minutes \ Servings: 1)

INGREDIENTS:

1 egg
1 bun, cut from top
1 pinch salt
¼ teaspoon dill, chopped

1 tablespoon red bell pepper, chopped
2 tablespoons olive oil

DIRECTIONS:

- Brush the bin with oil and crack the egg inside it.
- Sprinkle salt, dill and red bell pepper.
- Transfer to the Mueller pressure cooker and cook on EGG mode for 10 minutes.
- Top with the cap of the bun.

Hot Scrambled Egg

(Time: 15 minutes \ Servings: 2)

INGREDIENTS:

4 eggs, whisked
¼ teaspoon salt
1 cup chicken broth

¼ teaspoon black pepper
¼ teaspoon dill, chopped
2 tablespoons olive oil

DIRECTIONS:

- Heat oil in the Mueller pressure cooker on SAUTÉ mode and pour the whisked eggs.
- Crumble the eggs using a fork and add the chicken broth. Season with salt and pepper.
- When the chicken broth is dried out, transfer the scrambled eggs to a serving dish and top with dill.

Peanut Slabs

(Time: 35 minutes \ Servings: 4)

INGREDIENTS:

1 cup peanuts, roughly chopped
1 cup all-purpose flour
¼ cup caster sugar
¼ cup butter
1 cup strawberry jam
¼ cup almonds, sliced
½ teaspoon baking powder
¼ teaspoon salt

DIRECTIONS:

- In a bowl, add the flour, sugar, baking powder, salt, almonds, and peanuts and mix well.
- Beat the butter until fluffy and stir in the flour mixture.
- Now take a greased baking dish and spread half of the flour mixture on the bottom and press very well using the back of a spoon.
- Spread strawberry jam.
- Now spread the remaining flour mixture on top and press lightly with spoon.
- Place a trivet in the Mueller pressure cooker and place the dish on top.
- Cook on MANUAL mode for 25 minutes.

Blueberries and Cream with Oats

(Time: 20 Minutes \ Servings: 4)

INGREDIENTS

1 tbsp. of coconut oil
1 cup of steel cut oats
2 tbsp. of coconut sugar
1 tsp. of vanilla
1 pinch of salt

1 ½ cups of coconut milk
1 ½ cups of water
¾ cup of dried blueberries
1 tbsp. of chia seeds

FOR THE TOPPING:

Use cream and a little bit of milk.

½ cup of fresh blueberries

DIRECTIONS

- Select Sauté/Browning on the Mueller pressure cooker and let it heat.
- Add the coconut oil, and when it melts, add the oats and keep stirring for 5 minutes.
- Add the rest of the ingredients except for the fresh blueberries.
- Now, lock the lid and close tightly the pressure valve.
- Cook on a MANUAL mode for around 10 minutes.
- When you hear the timer, release the pressure after 10 minutes and press the quick release. Stir the ingredients and serve in bowls.
- You can add the cream and the fresh blueberries.

Scotch Rolls

(Time: 20 Minutes \ Servings: 5)

INGREDIENTS

4 large eggs
1 lb. of ground sausage
1 tbsp. of vegetable oil
1 tbsp. of coconut oil

½ lb. of cauliflower florets
½ cup of oat flour
1 tsp. of ginger
1 tsp. of flaxseed powder

DIRECTIONS

- Place the steamer basket in the Mueller pressure cooker.
- Add 1 cup of water and the eggs.
- After that, lock the lid and cook the eggs for 6 minutes on EGG mode.
- When the timer goes off, release the pressure naturally for around 5 minutes.
- When the pressure is completely released, carefully remove the lid.
- Chop the sausage into 4 pieces of equal size.
- Flatten each of the pieces until flat and round. Then put the hard - boiled eggs in the center and wrap the sausage around each egg.
- Heat the Mueller pressure cooker and press the function SAUTÉ for 10 to 15 minutes, and when the Pot is hot, add to it the oil and let the scotch eggs get a brown color and remove them.
- Place the rack in the Mueller pressure cooker and line the egg rolls on that rack; then lock the lid and set the timer to 6 minutes on EGG mode.
- Finally, remove the scotch eggs and enjoy them.

Cut Oats Breakfast

(Time: 35 Minutes \ Servings: 3-4)

INGREDIENTS

2 cups of cut oats
2 cups of coconut milk
1 cup of yogurt
3 cups of water
4 apples, diced
1 ½ cups of fresh cranberries
3 tbsp. of butter or coconut oil

1 tsp. of fresh lemon juice
½ tsp. of nutmeg
¼ cup of maple syrup
½ tsp. of salt
2 tsp. of vanilla
3 strawberries

DIRECTIONS

- Start by greasing the bottom of the Mueller pressure cooker container and add the butter or the coconut oil.
- Soak all ingredients except the maple syrup, the salt, and the vanilla and leave them overnight in the Mueller pressure cooker.
- The next morning, add the quantity of syrup and the salt and cook on porridge setting. Make sure to seal the valve.
- Set the timer to 15 minutes to reach MANUAL high pressure, then add 20 more minutes to cook the ingredients.
- Once the timer beeps, open the valve to release the pressure.
- Serve with milk, vanilla, and strawberries.

Ginger Quiche

(Time: 30 Minutes \ Servings: 3)

INGREDIENTS

6 Well beaten large eggs
½ cup of coconut milk
¼ tsp. of salt
¼ tsp. of ground black pepper
4 slices of bacon, cooked and
    crumbled

1 cup of cooked ground sausage
½ cup of diced salmon
2 green chopped onions
1 cup of shredded cheese
1 ½ tsp. of ground ginger
½ tsp. of flax seeds

DIRECTIONS

- Start by placing a metal trivet on the bottom of the Mueller pressure cooker and pour in 1 ½ cups of water.
- In a bowl, whisk together the milk, eggs, salt, and pepper.
- Then add the bacon, the sausage, the ham, the green onions, and the cheese to a 1-quart soufflé dish and mix very well.
- Pour the egg mixture above the meat and stir altogether to combine the ingredients.
- Now, cover the soufflé tray using the aluminum foil and sling to place it on top of the trivet on the pressure cooking pot. After that, lock the lid and set on MANUAL mode and time to 30 minutes.
- When the timer beeps, turn off the Mueller pressure cooker and wait for around 10 minutes, then apply the quick pressure release. Serve with cheese.

Benedict Asparagus with Eggs

(Time: 20 Minutes \ Servings: 2-3)

INGREDIENTS

7 stalks of asparagus
5 eggs
2 tsp. of apple cider vinegar
chives for garnishing
2 tbsp. hollandaise sauce

2 egg yolks
¼ cup of coconut oil
2 tsp. of fresh lemon juice
¼ tsp. of paprika
¼ tsp. of sea salt

DIRECTIONS

- Heat the Mueller pressure cooker and place the trivet inside it. Break each of the eggs into a small ramekin. Trim the asparagus stalks from the bottom.
- Slice the asparagus stalks lengthwise. Pour 1 cup of water into a sauce pan and cook the asparagus for 5 minutes.
- Place asparagus in each ramekin and add the cider vinegar. Slide the eggs in the ramekin, then cover the Mueller pressure cooker with a lid and set to SOUP mode, cooking the ingredients for 8 minutes.

- Prepare the sauce by boiling water in a blender, then cover and set aside for 10 minutes. Blend the egg yolk and add the lemon juice, the salt, and the paprika.
- Add the melted butter and keep mixing for 40 seconds. Serve each of the eggs over the dish of asparagus stalks and top with the hollandaise sauce and chives.

Coconut Yogurt with Blueberries

(Time: 10 hours \ Servings: 6)

INGREDIENTS

2 lb. of coconut milk
2 tsp. of agar flakes
4 tbsp. of coconut yogurt

2 tbsp. of raw sugar
1 cup of blueberries
½ cup of strawberries

DIRECTIONS

- Pour the coconut milk into a cooking pot. Whisk the milk until it smoothens and add the thickener; then sprinkle 1 tsp. of the agar flakes into the pot.
- Warm the coconut milk. Set to MANUAL and the timer to 5 minutes or until the milk begins simmering. Whisk from time to time until you notice the agar agar are dissolved. Turn off the heat.
- Add the probiotics and whisk to combine the ingredients. Add the sugar and whisk the ingredients again.
- Add the blueberries and the strawberries on top and don't stir. Lock the Pressure Valve. Use a lid made of glass. Press the YOGURT button. The program will automatically finish. Let cool before serving.

Raspberry and Oatmeal Pudding

(Time: 5 minutes \ Servings: 2)

INGREDIENTS

2 cups of water
½ tsp. of sea salt
1 cup of oats
½ cup of jujubes, diced into pieces

½ cup of raspberries
3 tbsp. of hemp seeds
1 tbsp. of dried flax seed powder
¼ cup of almond slivers

DIRECTIONS

- Pour the water and the salt into the Mueller pressure cooker and set to OATMEAL mode for 5 minutes.
- Once cooked, add the jujubes and the raspberries.
- Add the hemp seeds and the flax seed powder to the oatmeal.
- Cook for 1 more minute.
- Once the ingredients become consistent and mixed well, serve and enjoy with hemp milk.

Lunch Recipes

Mushroom Mix Recipe

(Time: 18 minutes \ Servings: 2)

INGREDIENTS:

2 tomatoes, chopped
½ lb. chicken, cooked and mashed
1 cup broccoli, chopped
1 tbsp. butter

2 tbsp. mayonnaise
½ cup mushroom soup
salt and pepper, to taste
1 onion, sliced

DIRECTIONS:

- Put chicken into a bowl.
- Mix mayonnaise, mushroom soup, tomatoes, onion, broccoli, and salt and pepper.
- Grease a round baking tray with butter. Put the mixture in a tray.
- Cook in the pressure cooker for 14 minutes on POULTRY mode.
- When ready, serve and enjoy!

Halibut Fillets

(Time: 15 minutes \ Servings: 2)

INGREDIENTS:

2 halibut fillets
1 tbsp. dill
1 tbsp. onion powder
1 cup parsley

2 tbsp. paprika
1 tbsp. garlic powder
1 tbsp. lemon pepper
2 tbsp. lemon juice

DIRECTIONS:

- Mix lemon juice, lemon pepper, garlic powder, and paprika, parsley and onion powder in a bowl.
- Add dill to it. Pour the mixture in the mueller pressure cooker and place halibut fish over it. Cook for 10 minutes on POULTRY mode.

Salmon with Soy Sauce

(Time: 15 minutes \ Servings: 3)

INGREDIENTS:

2 Salmon fillets
½ maple syrup
2 tbsp. soy sauce

1 tbsp. garlic powder
salt and pepper, to taste

DIRECTIONS:

- Put maple syrup, soy sauce, salt, pepper and garlic powder into a bowl.
- Dip salmon in the mixture and place it in the mueller pressure cooker. Cook for 15 minutes on STEAM mode.

Simple Salmon Cooked Recipe

(Time: 10 minutes \ Servings: 3)

INGREDIENTS:

1 lb. salmon, cooked, mashed
2 eggs
2 onions
2 stalks celery

1 cup parsley, chopped
1 tbsp. oil
salt and pepper, to taste

DIRECTIONS:

- Mix salmon, onion, celery, parsley, and salt and pepper in a bowl. Put oil in the mueller pressure cooker and let it sauté.
- Meanwhile, make patties out of the mixture and dip them in the whisked eggs.
- Place each patty in the pot when all are made, and cook them for 5 minutes on STEAM mode.
- When ready, serve the delicious fish patties.

Simply Cooked Shrimp

(Time: 13 minutes \ Servings: 2)

INGREDIENTS:

1 lb. shrimp
2 garlic cloves
2 tbsp. oil
1 tbsp. butter.

red pepper, a pinch
salt and pepper, to taste
1 cup parsley, chopped

DIRECTIONS:

- Put the shrimp into the mueller pressure cooker and brown them for 2 minutes on SAUTÉ mode .
- Add garlic cloves, oil, butter, red pepper, and salt and pepper. Cook for another 5 minutes on STEAM.
- When ready, release the pressure and garnish with parsley before serving.

Delicious Crab Meat Recipe

(Time: 15 minutes \ Servings: 3)

INGREDIENTS:

1 lb. crab meat
½ cup cream cheese
2 tbsp. mayonnaise

salt and pepper, to taste
1 tbsp. lemon juice
1 cup cheese, shredded

DIRECTIONS:

- Mix mayonnaise, cream cheese, salt and pepper, and lemon juice in a bowl.
- Add crab meat to it and make small balls.
- Place the balls in the mueller pressure cooker and let them cook for 10 minutes on STEAM mode.
- When done, sprinkle the cheese over before serving.

Tilapia Delight

(Time: 16 minutes \ Servings: 4)

INGREDIENTS:

4 tilapia fillets
4 tbsp. lemon juice
2 tbsp. butter

2 garlic cloves
½ cup parsley
salt and pepper, to taste

DIRECTIONS:

- Mix tilapia with lemon juice and put it into the mueller pressure cooker.
- Add butter, garlic cloves, parsley, and sprinkle salt and pepper over it.
- Close the lid and cook for 10 minutes on STEAM mode.
- When ready, serve and enjoy this simple tilapia recipe.

Sweet Potato with Cheese

(Time: 15 minutes \ Servings: 3)

INGREDIENTS:

2 lb. sweet potatoes, cubed
2 garlic cloves
1 tbsp. sage
1 tbsp. rosemary

2 tbsp. butter
2 cups grated cheese
Salt to taste

DIRECTIONS:

- Add garlic cloves into the mueller pressure cooker along with sage, butter and rosemary.
- Add sweet potatoes with salt. Cook on BEANS mode for 10 minutes.
- When ready, enjoy the tasty meal!

Spinach Mix Tomatoes

(Time: 14 minutes \ Servings: 2)

INGREDIENTS:

2 tbsp. butter
1 onion, chopped
2 cloves garlic – 2 cloves
1 tbsp. cumin powder
1 tbsp. paprika

2 tomatoes , chopped
2 cups vegetable broth
1 small bunch of spinach, chopped
cilantro for garnishing

DIRECTIONS:

- Add butter into the mueller pressure cooker. Sauté it. Mix onion, garlic, and cumin powder, paprika, and vegetable broth. Stir well.
- Add tomatoes and spinach. Cook on BEANS mode for 10 minutes.

Black Beans with Lentils and Veggies

(Time: 15 minutes \ Servings: 2)

INGREDIENTS:

1 tbsp. olive oil
1 red onion , chopped
2 carrots , chopped
1 tbsp. oregano
2 tbsp. garlic powder

2 tomatoes , chopped
1 cup water
1 cup lentils
4 cups black beans
salt to taste

DIRECTIONS:

- Add oil into the mueller pressure cooker and let it sauté.
- Mix together red onion, black beans, lentils, water, tomatoes, garlic powder, oregano and carrots.
- Add the mixture to the pot.
- Let it cook for 10 minutes on BEANS mode.

Black Beans Chicken Mix

(Time: 20 minutes \ Servings: 3)

INGREDIENTS:

1 tbsp. olive oil
2 cups chicken breast, cubed
1 green bell pepper
3 cups black beans
1 tbsp. cumin powder
2 cups cabbage leaves
1 tbsp. garlic powder

1 tbsp. cayenne powder
salt to taste

DIRECTIONS:

- Add oil into the mueller pressure cooker and let it sauté.
- Mix chicken cubes, cumin powder and cayenne powder in a bowl. Mix well.
- Add the chicken mixture to the mueller pressure cooker along with the bell pepper, black beans, cabbage leaves and garlic powder.
- Salt to taste. Cook on BEANS mode for 15 minutes.
- When done, serve and enjoy the meal!

Black-Eyed Peas

(Time: 15 minutes \ Servings: 2)

INGREDIENTS:

2 sweet potatoes, sliced
1 tbsp. coriander seeds
1 tbsp. cumin seeds
black-eyed peas

salt to taste
2 garlic cloves
2 cups tomato paste
1 onion, chopped

DIRECTIONS:

- Add tomato paste into the mueller pressure cooker.
- Stir slowly.
- Mix onion, garlic, salt, black-eyed peas, cumin seeds and coriander seeds.
- Add sweet potatoes.
- Cook for 10 minutes on BEANS mode.

Rice Mixed Beans

(Time: 15 minutes \ Servings: 3)

INGREDIENTS:

1 onion , diced
2 garlic cloves
2 cups brown rice
2 cups black beans

3 cups water
salt to taste
1 avocado, cubed

DIRECTIONS:

- Add water into the pressure cooker with the black beans and rice.
- Cook for 4 minutes.
- Add garlic, salt and avocado. Cook on BEANS mode for 15 minutes.

Borlotti Beans with Tomato Sauce

(Time: 16 minutes \ Servings: 3)

INGREDIENTS:

2 cups Tomato sauce
2 tbsp. Oregano powder
1 tbsp. Red pepper flakes
1 Carrot, sliced

2 Garlic cloves
1 Onion , chopped
2 cups Borlotti beans
salt to taste

DIRECTIONS:

- Add tomato sauce with oregano powder into the pressure cooker.
- Mix in the carrot, red pepper flakes, garlic, onion, beans and salt.
- Cook for 10 minutes on BEANS mode. When ready, serve and enjoy!

White Beans Recipe

(Time: 16 minutes \ Servings: 3)

INGREDIENTS:

1 tbsp. olive oil
2 tbsp. garlic, minced
2 cups spinach
2 tomatoes

3 cups white beans
salt and pepper, to taste
cheese to garnish

DIRECTIONS:

- Add oil into the pressure cooker and sauté it.
- Add garlic, spinach, tomatoes, white beans and salt and pepper. Mix well.
- Cook for 10 minutes on high pressure on BEANS mode.
- When ready, garnish with cheese before serving.

Black Beans with Tomatoes

(Time: 14 minutes \ Servings: 3)

INGREDIENTS:

2 tbsp. canola oil
1 onion, chopped
1 zucchini, chopped
3 cups black beans

2 tomatoes, diced
salt and pepper, to taste
½ cup corn
parsley to garnish

DIRECTIONS:

- Add oil into the pressure cooker.
- Mix onion, black beans, tomatoes, corn, zucchini, and salt and pepper.
- Cook for 10 minutes on BEANS mode.
- When done, garnish with parsley and serve.

Beans with Chickpeas

(Time: 18 minutes \ Servings: 3)

INGREDIENTS:

3 cups red kidney beans
3 cups chickpeas
1 tbsp. curry powder
1 tbsp. black pepper
1 tbsp. oil

Salt to taste
1 tbsp. mustard seeds
2 cloves garlic, minced
1 cup water

DIRECTIONS:

- Add oil into the pressure cooker. Add chickpeas and stir well.
- Mix in the curry powder, mustard seeds, kidney beans, garlic, water and black pepper.
- Cook on MULTIGRAIN mode for 15 minutes.
- When ready, serve and enjoy!

Cheesy Macaroni

(Time: 30 minutes \ Servings: 3)

INGREDIENTS:

1 package macaroni
half lb. mozzarella cheese
¼ cup cream cheese
1 cup parmesan cheese
2-3 garlic cloves

¼ teaspoon black pepper
¼ teaspoon salt
½ cup vegetable broth
2 tablespoons butter

DIRECTIONS:

- Set the Pressure cooker on sauté mode and melt butter.
- Sauté garlic for 30 seconds and add the vegetable broth.
- Add in the the macaroni, mozzarella cheese, parmesan cheese and cream cheese.
- Season with salt and pepper.
- Cover the pot with a lid and cook on high pressure MANUAL mode for 30 minutes.

Lemony Chicken Pasta

(Time: 35 minutes \ Servings: 3)

INGREDIENTS:

1 package pasta, boiled
¼ lb. chicken, breasts
4 tablespoons lemon juice
½ cup ketchup
2 tablespoons olive oil

DIRECTIONS:

- Heat oil in the Pressure cooker on SAUTÉ mode. Add the chicken and fry until golden brown.
- Add the pasta and fry for 3-4 minutes. Now add the ketchup and mix well.
- Cook for another 4-5 minutes.
- Turn off the heat and transfer to a serving dish.
- Drizzle lemon juice and serve.

Lamb with Thyme

(Time: 55 minutes \ Servings: 4)

INGREDIENTS:

½ lb. lamb, pieces
2 carrots, sliced
3 tablespoons thyme springs

1 teaspoon salt
3 cups water
8 oz. boiled rice, optional

DIRECTIONS:

- In the Pressure cooker add the lamb pieces, carrots, thyme, salt and water.
- Cover and cook on MEAT mode for 50 minutes.
- Serve with the boiled rice or bread.

Lamb Loin Dish

(Time: 18 minutes \ Servings: 3)

INGREDIENTS:

2 tbsp. butter
4 pieces lamb loin
2 carrots, chopped
2 cups lamb stock

2 cups baby spinach
2 Garlic cloves, minced
salt and pepper, to taste

DIRECTIONS:

- Add butter into the pressure cooker. Select SAUTÉ and heat it.
- Mix in the carrots, lamb stock, baby spinach, garlic cloves, and salt and pepper. Cook for 4 minutes.
- Add lamb loin and cook for another 12 minutes on MEAT mode.

Roasted Turkey

(Time: 50 minutes \ Servings: 4)

INGREDIENTS:

t1 white turkey
1 teaspoon garlic paste

¼ teaspoon salt
¼ teaspoon chili powder

½ teaspoon black pepper
¼ teaspoon thyme
¼ teaspoon rosemary
½ teaspoon cinnamon powder

3 tablespoons lemon juice
4 tablespoons orange juice
3 tablespoons olive oil

DIRECTIONS:

- In a bowl combine orange juice, lemon juice, thyme, rosemary, garlic paste salt, pepper, chili powder, olive oil, and cinnamon powder, mix well.
- Pour on the turkey and rub with hands.
- Transfer the turkey to a greased Pressure cooker and cover with a lid.
- Cook on MEAT mode for 45-50 minutes.

Cellini Beans with Baby Broccoli and Carrots

(Time: 30 minutes \ Servings: 5)

INGREDIENTS:

2 cup Cellini beans, soaked
2 carrots, sliced
1 cup broccoli florets
¼ teaspoon salt

½ teaspoon white pepper
2 tablespoons lemon juice
3 cups chicken broth
3 tablespoons olive oil

DIRECTIONS:

- In the Pressure cooker, add the Cellini beans, carrots, broccoli, salt, pepper, lemon juice, chicken broth, and olive oil, stir and cover with a lid.
- Cook on BEANS mode for 30 minutes.

Broccoli Pasta

(Time: 35 minutes \ Servings: 3)

INGREDIENTS:

1 package pasta
1 cup broccoli florets
1 teaspoon garlic paste
¼ teaspoon salt
1 cup vegetable broth

¼ teaspoon white pepper
2 cups chicken broth
2 tablespoons lemon juice
2 tablespoons olive oil

DIRECTIONS:

- In the Pressure cooker, add garlic and oil and sauté for 1 minute on sauté mode.
- Add the broccoli and stir well.
- Pour in the chicken broth with the pasta and mix well.
- Season with salt and pepper.
- Cover with a lid and cook on MANUAL mode for 30 minutes.

Hot Red Beans Curry

(Time: 50 minutes \ Servings: 5)

INGREDIENTS:

1 cup red beans, soaked overnight
2 tomatoes, chopped
1 medium onion, chopped
1 teaspoon garlic paste
¼ teaspoon turmeric powder
¼ teaspoon salt
¼ teaspoon chili powder

¼ teaspoon cinnamon powder
½ teaspoon cumin powder
2 cups chicken broth
2 cups water
1 green chili
2 tablespoons olive oil

DIRECTIONS:

- Add the water and the red beans and boil for 20 minutes on SOUP cook mode.
- Drain the beans and set aside.
- Heat oil in the Pressure cooker on sauté mode and add onion.
- Fry until transparent.
- Add garlic, tomatoes, salt, chili powder, turmeric powder and fry for 5 minutes.
- Now add the red beans and stir-fry for 5 minutes.
- Stir in the chicken broth and the green chili.
- Cover with a lid and cook on CHILI mode for 20 minutes.
- Sprinkle cumin powder and cinnamon powder.

Black Lentils

(Time: 45 minutes \ Servings: 5)

INGREDIENTS:

1 cup black lentils, soaked overnight
2 tomatoes, chopped
1 teaspoon garlic paste
¼ teaspoon ginger paste
¼ teaspoon turmeric powder
¼ teaspoon salt

¼ teaspoon chili powder
2 cups chicken broth
2 cups water
2 tablespoons olive oil
1 avocado, for garnishing

DIRECTIONS:

- Add the water, lentils, turmeric powder, and chili powder and boil for 30 minutes on MANUAL cook mode.
- Now transfer the lentils and the stew to a bowl and set aside.
- Heat oil in the Pressure cooker on sauté mode and add garlic and ginger. Fry for 30 seconds.
- Add the tomatoes, and the salt and fry for 5-6 minutes.
- Stir in the lentils and the chicken broth. Cook on BEANS mode for 15 minutes.

Spinach Orzo

(Time: 40 minutes \ Servings: 4)

INGREDIENTS:

1 cup white orzo
1 cup baby spinach, chopped
1 cup cream cheese
¼ teaspoon black pepper

½ teaspoon salt
2-3 garlic cloves, chopped
2 cups vegetable broth
2 tablespoons cooking oil

DIRECTIONS:

- Set the Pressure cooker on sauté mode and heat oil.
- Sauté garlic for 30 seconds.
- Add the orzo, spinach, salt and pepper and cook for 1-2 minutes.
- Now add the chicken broth, stir well.
- Cover with a lid and cook for 35 minutes on SLOW COOK mode.
- Add the cream cheese and cook for another 5 minutes on low heat.

Chili Garlic Eggplant Pasta

(Time: 30 minutes \ Servings: 3)

INGREDIENTS:

16 oz. package of pasta
1 large egg plant, sliced
1 cup chili garlic sauce
2 tablespoons barbecue sauce
½ cup ketchup

¼ teaspoon chili powder
2-3 garlic cloves, chopped
2 cups vegetable broth
2 tablespoons cooking oil

DIRECTIONS:

- Set the Pressure cooker on sauté mode and heat oil.
- Fry garlic for 30 seconds.
- Add the eggplants and fry until golden.
- Transfer the eggplants to a separate bowl and set aside.
- Now in the Pressure cooker, add the chili garlic sauce, ketchup, chili powder, barbecue sauce, and vegetable broth, stir well.
- Add the pasta and cook for 20 minutes on CHILI mode.
- Then add the eggplants and mix thoroughly.
- Cook for another minute.

Cottage Cabbage Macaroni

(Time: 25 minutes \ Servings: 3)

INGREDIENTS:

16 oz. package of macaroni
1 cup cabbage, copped
1 cup cottage cheese, shredded
2-3 garlic cloves, chopped

¼ teaspoon salt
¼ teaspoon white pepper
2 cups vegetable broth
2 tablespoons cooking oil

DIRECTIONS:

- Set the Pressure cooker on sauté mode, heat oil and fry garlic for 30 seconds.
- Add the cabbage and fry for 1-2 minutes.
- Add the vegetable broth, macaroni, salt, pepper, and cheese and cover up with a lid.
- Cook for 20 minutes on MANUAL mode.

Slow Cooked Spiced Cabbage

(Time: 60 minutes \ Servings: 2)

INGREDIENTS:

1 cabbage, halved
¼ teaspoon salt
½ teaspoon thyme
¼ teaspoon black pepper

1 tablespoon soya sauce
1 teaspoon garlic powder
2 tablespoons olive oil

DIRECTIONS:

- In a bowl, combine the soya sauce, salt, pepper, thyme, garlic powder and olive oil.
- Place the cabbage into the greased Pressure cooker.
- Pour the mixture from the bowl over the cabbage.
- Cover the pot and set to SLOW COOK mode for 60 minutes.

Snacks and Appetizers

Potatoes and Black Beans

(Time: 16 minutes \ Servings: 3)

INGREDIENTS:

2 tbsp. olive oil
1 sweet potato, sliced
1 onion , diced
2 tbsp. chili powder
1 tbsp. cumin powder

salt to taste
3 cups black beans
cilantro to garnish
2 tbsp. red hot sauce

DIRECTIONS:

- Add oil into the pressure cooker and sauté it.
- Mix in the onion, red hot sauce, black beans, salt, cumin powder, and chili powder.
- Stir well.
- Add sweet potatoes and cook on BEANS mode for 10 minutes.
- When done, garnish with cilantro and serve!
-

Sweet Potatoes with Cheese

(Time: 15 minutes \ Servings: 4)

INGREDIENTS:

4 sweet potatoes, diced
3 garlic cloves, chopped
salt and pepper, to taste
½ cup parsley, chopped
½ cup sage, chopped

½ cup thyme, chopped
½ cup milk
2 tbsp. butter
½ cup shredded cheese

DIRECTIONS:

- Add sweet potatoes, salt and pepper, garlic cloves, sage, parsley, thyme and milk into the Pressure cooker.
- Cook for 10 minutes on MANUAL mode, high pressure.
- Release the pressure and then add butter and cheese to it.
- Cook for another 5 minutes.
- When ready, serve and enjoy!

Simple Rice Recipe

(Time: 10 minutes \ Servings: 4)

INGREDIENTS:

4 cups Pink rice, uncooked
5 cups Water

½ tbsp. Salt

DIRECTIONS:

- Add water into the pressure cooker and mix in the rice and salt.
- Let it cook on RICE mode for 15 minutes.
- When ready, serve and enjoy with any dish.
- If you wish to garnish it, you can do it with any of your favorite ingredients!

Rice with Saffron

(Time: 11 minutes \ Servings: 3)

INGREDIENTS:

½ tsp. saffron threads
2 tbsp. milk
½ tbsp. olive oil
1 onion, chopped
½ cup rice, uncooked

2 cups vegetable broth
2 cinnamon stick
salt to taste
chopped almonds for seasoning

DIRECTIONS:

- Add onion, vegetable broth, salt, cinnamon stick, olive oil and saffron threads into the Pressure cooker.
- Let it cook for 2 minutes.
- Add rice to it along with milk.
- Cook on RICE mode for 15 minutes.
- When ready, serve with chopped almonds on top.

Ripe Plantain Cheesy Patty

(Time: 12 minutes \ Servings: 2)

INGREDIENTS:

2 large ripe plantains
Oil for frying

8 mozzarella cheese slices

FOR THE BATTER

2 Eggs
4 tbsp. all-purpose flour
2 tbsp. sugar

2 tbsp. milk
a pinch of salt

DIRECTIONS:

- Add oil into the pressure cooker.
- Mix ripe plantain and cheese in a bowl.
- Make round patties out of the mixture.
- Set aside.
- Prepare the batter: mix eggs, flour, sugar, milk and salt in another bowl.
- Dip the plantain patties into the batter.
- Place in the pot.
- Cook for 10 minutes on MANUAL mode.
- When ready, serve and enjoy!

Ritz Shrimp Snack

(Time: 17 minutes \ Servings: 2)

INGREDIENTS:

2 tbsp. oil
2 garlic cloves, minced
2 tbsp. red pepper flakes.
salt and pepper, to taste
1 lb. shrimp

2 avocados, diced
juice from 1 lime
1 cup cilantro leaves, chopped
12 Ritz crackers
1 cup queso fresco crumbles

DIRECTIONS:

- Add oil into the pressure cooker.
- Mix in the garlic cloves, shrimp and red pepper flakes.
- Stir well.
- Cook for 10 minutes on STEAM mode.
- Add mashed avocados and lime juice.
- Cook for another 5 minutes.
- When ready, set aside.
- Place the Ritz crackers on a plate.
- Add avocado mixture and top it with the shrimp.
- Garnish with queso fresco crumbles to serve and enjoy!

Avocado Paste Snack

(Time: 25 minutes \ Servings: 2)

INGREDIENTS:

2 avocados
¼ cup green bell pepper, diced
2 cup cucumber, diced
salt and pepper, to taste

2 tbsp. lime juice
2 tbsp. cilantro
1 cup water
¼ cup white vinegar

DIRECTIONS:

- Add avocados and green bell pepper into the pot.
- Mix in the cucumber and water.
- Cook for 5 minutes.
- Blend the mixture in an electric blender for 2 minutes.
- Put the mixture back into the same pot.
- Mix in lime juice, white vinegar, and salt and pepper.
- Cook for another 15 minutes on CHILI mode.
- When ready, garnish with cilantro to serve!

Delicious Chorizo Snack

(Time: 12 minutes \ Servings: 2)

INGREDIENTS:

2 cups cornmeal
3 tbsp. oil
2 tbsp. parmesan cheese
2 tbsp. butter

a pinch of salt
1 cup fresco crumbles
2 chorizos, sliced and cooked
cilantro for garnish

DIRECTIONS:

- Mix together cornmeal and parmesan cheese in a bowl.
- Add butter and salt. Mix well.
- Make small patties out of the mixture.
- Add oil into the Pressure cooker.
- Place patties in pressure cooker and cook for 5 minutes on CHILI mode.
- When ready, set aside.
- Place chorizo slices on the plate.
- Add fresco crumbles, then place a patty on top.
- Garnish with cilantro and serve!

Tomatoes Mix Recipe

(Time: 10 minutes \ Servings: 3)

INGREDIENTS:

1 tbsp. olive oil
1 onion, chopped
2 garlic cloves, minced
2 cup vegetable stock
2 tomatoes, diced

salt to taste
2 bay leaf
½ tbsp. oregano powder
½ tbsp. rosemary powder.
¼ cup basil

DIRECTIONS:

- Add olive oil in the pressure cooker and press the sauté button.
- Mix onion, tomatoes, vegetable stock, bay leaf, rosemary powder, salt, and oregano powder.
- Let it cook on VEGETABLE mode for 5 minutes.
- When ready, serve with basil over it. Enjoy!

Sweet Potatoes with Butter and Vanilla

(Time: 15 minutes \ Servings: 4)

INGREDIENTS:

3 sweet potatoes, diced
½ tbsp. sugar
1 tbsp. butter
½ tbsp. vanilla

1 tbsp. cinnamon powder
1 tbsp. nutmeg powder
2 cups heavy cream

DIRECTIONS:

- Add sweet potatoes along with sugar, vanilla, butter, nutmeg and cinnamon powder into the Pressure cooker.
- Cook on VEGETABLE mode for 10 minutes.
- When ready, dress with heavy cream and serve!

Quinoa with Vegetables

(Time: 10 minutes \ Servings: 4)

INGREDIENTS:

½ cup quinoa
1 cup water
1 carrot, sliced
1 cucumber, sliced
½ cup frozen edamame

2 onions, sliced
½ cabbage, chopped
½ tbsp. soy sauce
½ tbsp. ginger, minced
salt to taste

DIRECTIONS:

- Add quinoa, salt, water, cucumber, edamame, carrot, cabbage and onion into the pressure cooker.
- Cook for 5 minutes on MANUAL mode.
- Mix soy sauce and ginger in a bowl.
- When the pot beeps, serve the quinoa and pour the sauce over it.

Potatoes with Parsley

(Time: 13 minutes \ Servings: 3)

INGREDIENTS:

4 potatoes, diced
2 cups of water
2 eggs
1 onion, chopped
2 tbsp. mayonnaise

½ cup Parsley, chopped
½ cup dill pickle juice
1 tbsp. mustard
salt and pepper, to taste

DIRECTIONS:

- Add water and potatoes in the mueller pressure cooker. Cook on high pressure for 3 minutes. Whisk the eggs and add them to the pot.
- Add onion, parsley, dill pickle juice, mayonnaise, mustard, salt and pepper.
- Mix well. Cook on VEGETABLE mode for 5 minutes.

Cauliflower Onion Mix Recipe

(Time: 15 minutes \ Servings: 3)

INGREDIENTS:

4 cups cauliflower florets
2 tbsp. olive oil
salt and pepper, to taste
2 onion, diced
3 cloves garlic, minced

2 cups chicken broth
1 tbsp. thyme , chopped
1 tbsp. butter
½ bunch parsley, chopped

DIRECTIONS:

- Mix olive oil with salt and pepper into the mueller pressure cooker.
- Add cauliflower florets. Add onion, chicken broth, garlic, thyme and butter.
- Cook it on VEGETABLE mode for 15 minutes.
- Release the pressure and take it out. Serve with parsley seasoning on it.

Simple Potato Recipe

(Time: 15 minutes \ Servings: 4)

INGREDIENTS:

4 potatoes, diced
2 tbsp. olive oil

2 garlic cloves, minced
2 tbsp. rosemary, chopped

DIRECTIONS:

- Add olive oil with potatoes into the mueller pressure cooker.
- Put garlic cloves and rosemary in the pot and cook for 10 minutes on MANUAL mode. When done, serve in a bowl and enjoy!

Simple Fries

(Time: 15 minutes \ Servings: 4)

INGREDIENTS:

2 potatoes, sliced
1 tbsp. flour
½ cup parsley, chopped

2 tbsp. oil
salt and pepper, to taste

DIRECTIONS:

- Put potatoes, flour, parsley, and salt and pepper into a bowl.
- Keep it aside.
- Add oil into the pressure cooker.
- Add the potatoes and cook for 14 minutes on MANUAL mode.
- When ready, serve and enjoy!

Coated Mozzarella Sticks

(Time: 35 minutes \ Servings: 6)

INGREDIENTS:

¼ lb. mozzarella cheese, cut into 1
   inch strips
1 teaspoon onion powder
1 cup bread crumbs
1 egg, whisked

1 teaspoon garlic powder
½ teaspoon salt
½ teaspoon chili powder
½ teaspoon cinnamon powder
1 cup oil, for frying

DIRECTIONS:

- In a bowl, combine bread crumbs, onion powder, salt, chili powder, garlic, cumin powder and toss well.
- Dip each mozzarella stick into the whisked egg and then roll out into the bread crumbs mixture.
- Heat oil in the Pressure cooker on SAUTÉ mode. Place the sticks inside the oil and fry until golden.
- Put them on a paper towel to drain out the excessive oil.
- Transfer to a serving dish and serve with any sauce.

Mushrooms and Pepper Mix

(Time: 16 minutes \ Servings: 2)

INGREDIENTS:

1 onion, chopped
1 green bell pepper, chopped
5 mushrooms, chopped

2 eggs
salt and pepper, to taste

DIRECTIONS:

- Whisk eggs in a bowl. Mix onion, green bell pepper, mushrooms, salt and pepper with the eggs.
- Blend well. Pour the mixture into a round baking tray.
- Let it cook in the pressure cooker for 10 minutes on MANUAL mode.
- When done, serve with bread or pitas to enjoy!

Sweet Potato Wedges

(Time: 25 minutes \ Servings: 4)

INGREDIENTS:

3 medium sweet potatoes, cut into wedges
1 teaspoon garlic powder
½ teaspoon salt
½ teaspoon black pepper
½ teaspoon cinnamon powder
½ teaspoon cumin powder
2 tablespoons lemon juice
1 cup oil, for frying

DIRECTIONS:

- In a bowl, combine salt, garlic, pepper, cumin powder, and cinnamon powder and toss.
- Set aside.
- Heat oil in the Pressure cooker on SAUTÉ mode.
- Transfer the sweet potatoes into the oil and fry until golden.
- Place on a paper towel. Season with salt and pepper.
- Transfer to a serving dish, drizzle some lemon juice on top and serve.

Potato Chips

(Time: 30 minutes \ Servings: 4)

INGREDIENTS:

4 potatoes, sliced for chips
¼ teaspoon salt
1 teaspoon thyme
¼ teaspoon black pepper
¼ garlic powder
½ cup cooking oil, for frying

DIRECTIONS:

- Heat oil in the Pressure cooker on SAUTÉ mode.
- Fry the potato slices until golden and crisp.
- Transfer to a paper towel and drain out excessive oil.
- Season with thyme, garlic powder, salt and pepper.

Greek-style fried Shrimp

(Time: 25 minutes \ Servings: 3)

INGREDIENTS:

2 oz. carrots, sliced
½ lb. shrimp
¼ teaspoon salt
¼ teaspoon black pepper

2 tablespoons lemon juice
1 teaspoon garlic powder
2 tablespoons oil, for frying

DIRECTIONS:

- Heat oil in the Pressure cooker on SAUTÉ mode.
- Add the shrimp and stir-fry for 10-15 minutes.
- Season with salt, garlic and pepper. Cook for another 10 minutes.
- Drizzle lemon juice and toss around.

Stir Fried Cherry Tomatoes

(Time: 15 minutes \ Servings: 4)

INGREDIENTS:

2 cups cherry tomatoes
¼ teaspoon salt
¼ teaspoon black pepper

3 tablespoons vinegar
2 tablespoons oil, for frying

DIRECTIONS:

- Heat oil in the Pressure cooker on SAUTÉ mode.
- Add the shrimp and sti- fry for 10-15 minutes.
- Season with salt and pepper.
- Add vinegar and toss.
- Cook for another 4 minutes.

Potato Wings

(Time: 35 minutes \ Servings: 6)

INGREDIENTS:

3 large potatoes, cut into wings
2 tablespoons gram flour
1 teaspoon garlic powder
½ teaspoon salt
½ teaspoon black pepper

½ teaspoon cinnamon powder
½ teaspoon cumin powder
2 tablespoons lemon juice
1 cup oil, for frying

DIRECTIONS:

- In a bowl, combine flour, salt, garlic, pepper, cumin powder, and cinnamon powder and toss.

- Add in the potato wings and toss. Heat oil in the Pressure cooker on SAUTÉ mode.
- Transfer the potatoes into the oil and fry until golden.
- Place on a paper towel to drain excess oil.
- Transfer to a serving dish, drizzle some lemon juice on top and serve.

Crispy Okra

(Time: 25 minutes \ Servings: 6)

INGREDIENTS:

½ lb. okra, heads removed
½ teaspoon salt

½ teaspoon black pepper
¼ cup oil, for frying

DIRECTIONS:

- Slice the okra lengthwise.
- Heat oil in the Pressure cooker on SAUTÉ mode.
- Transfer the okra into the oil and fry until golden.
- Place on a paper towel then season with salt and pepper.
- Transfer to a serving dish and enjoy.

Crispy Chicken Fritters

(Time: 25 minutes \ Servings: 4)

INGREDIENTS:

6 chicken breasts fillets
½ cup bread crumbs
1 teaspoon garlic powder
1 teaspoon onion powder
1 teaspoon dry coriander powder

1 teaspoon cumin powder
Oil spray
1 egg
1 teaspoon salt
½ teaspoon black pepper

DIRECTIONS:

- In a bowl, mix breadcrumbs with coriander powder, onion powder, cumin powder, salt, and black pepper and toss well.
- Roll each chicken fillet into the breadcrumbs; mixture and transfer into a platter.
- Place the chicken fillets into the Pressure cooker and cook on POULTRY mode for 20 minutes. Serve with tomato ketchup and enjoy.

Spiced Fried Cauliflower

(Time: 35 minutes \ Servings: 2)

INGREDIENTS:

1 cup cauliflower florets
1 teaspoon onion powder

1 cup all-purpose flour
1 teaspoon garlic powder

½ teaspoon salt
½ teaspoon chili powder

½ teaspoon cinnamon powder
1 cup oil, for frying

DIRECTIONS:

- In a bowl, combine flour, onion powder, salt, chili powder, garlic, and cumin powder, and toss.
- Add in cauliflower and mix well.
- Heat oil in Pressure cooker on SAUTÉ mode.
- Transfer the cauliflower into oil and fry until golden.
- Place on paper towel to drain out excess oil.
- Transfer to serving dish and serve with any sauce.

Creamy Mashed Potatoes

(Time: 30 minutes \ Servings: 3)

INGREDIENTS:

4 large potatoes, boiled and peeled
1 cup sour cream
½ cup heavy cream

1 pinch salt
¼ teaspoon black pepper

DIRECTIONS:

- Place the boiled potatoes, sour cream, and heavy cream into the Pressure cooker and cover with a lid.
- Cook on SLOW COOK mode for 30 minutes. Season with salt and pepper before mashing. Serve as garnish for meat or fish.

Chickpea Hummus

(Time: 60 minutes \ Servings: 4)

INGREDIENTS:

1 cup chickpea, soaked
1 pinch salt
¼ teaspoon chili powder

3 cups of water
2 tablespoons olive oil
2 garlic cloves, minced

DIRECTIONS:

- Transfer the water, chickpea, salt and garlic into the Pressure cooker.
- Set it on MULTIGRAIN.
- Cover with a lid and cook for 35 minutes.
- Let it cool a little, then transfer the boiled chickpea into a blender and blend to a puree.
- Add olive oil gradually and keep blending.
- Put on a serving dish and sprinkle chili powder on top.

Chicken Bites

(Time: 55 minutes \ Servings: 6)

INGREDIENTS:

2 chicken breast
4 tablespoons breadcrumbs
½ teaspoon salt
1 egg

1 teaspoon black pepper
1 teaspoon red paprika
1 bunch of parsley
2 tablespoons oil

DIRECTIONS:

- Cut the chicken breasts into small chunks.
- In a bowl, put the chicken breasts, sprinkle salt, black pepper, 1 egg and breadcrumbs.
- Add oil in the Pressure cooker and transfer the chicken to it.
- Set the cooker on CHICKEN mode and cook for 30 minutes.

Ginger Zest Pineapple Slices

(Time: 15 minutes \ Servings: 3)

INGREDIENTS:

2 cups pineapple slices
1 pinch salt
¼ teaspoon black pepper

1-inch ginger slice, chopped
1 teaspoon lemon juice
2 tablespoons oil

DIRECTIONS:

- Heat oil in the Pressure cooker and stir fry ginger for 1 minute on SAUTÉ mode.
- Add in pineapple and stir fry well, 3-4 minutes.
- Season with salt, and pepper.
- Drizzle lemon juice and toss well.

Vegetable and Eggs

Spinach and Potato Risotto

(Time: 45 minutes \ Servings: 5)

INGREDIENTS:

2 cups spinach, chopped
¼ cup mushrooms, sliced
2 large potatoes, peeled, diced
1 onion, chopped
2-3 cherry tomatoes, halved
½ teaspoon salt

¼ teaspoons turmeric powder
1 teaspoon chili flakes
½ teaspoon garlic paste
3 tablespoons cooking oil
2 cups water

DIRECTIONS:

- Heat oil in the Pressure cooker on SAUTÉ mode. Fry the onion until transparent.
- Add the mushrooms, garlic, salt, chili flakes, and turmeric powder and stir-fry.
- Now add the spinach, the water and the potatoes and cover with a lid.
- Cook on MANUAL mode for 35 minutes.
- Top with cherry tomatoes and cook for 1-2 minutes.

Zucchini Chips

(Time: 15 minutes \ Servings: 4)

INGREDIENTS:

3 large zucchinis, thinly sliced
¼ teaspoon salt

¼ teaspoon black pepper
½ tablespoons cooking oil, for frying

DIRECTIONS:

- Heat oil in the Pressure cooker on SAUTÉ mode.
- Put a few slices of zucchini in the Pressure cooker and fry until golden and crisp.
- Repeat the same steps for all zucchini chips.
- Then place onto a paper towel to drain out the excessive oil.

Garlicky Roasted Potatoes

(Time: 45 minutes \ Servings: 3)

INGREDIENTS:

3 large potatoes, cut, 1-inch slice
1 teaspoon garlic powder
1 teaspoon black pepper

1 teaspoon salt
4 tablespoons olive oil

DIRECTIONS:

- In a bowl, add olive oil, garlic powder, salt, and black pepper and mix.
- Add the potatoes and toss well.
- Transfer into the Pressure cooker and roast on MANUAL mode for 15-20 minutes.
- Serve hot and enjoy.

Cauliflower Carrot Risotto

(Time: 45 minutes \ Servings: 4)

INGREDIENTS:

1 cup cauliflower, florets
2 carrots, sliced
1 oz. tofu
1 onion, thinly sliced
1 teaspoon garlic paste

2 tomatoes, chopped
1 teaspoon black pepper
½ teaspoon salt
1 cup chicken broth
2 tablespoons cooking oil

DIRECTIONS:

- Set the Pressure cooker on MANUAL mode.
- Combine the cauliflower, carrots, tofu, tomatoes, onion, garlic paste, vegetable broth and cooking oil.
- Season with salt and black pepper.
- Cover and cook for 25 minutes on BEANS mode.

Pressure cooker Creamy Mushrooms

(Time: 25 minutes \ Servings: 3)

INGREDIENTS:

1 cup mushrooms, sliced
1 cup cream
½ cup cream cheese
¼ teaspoon black pepper

½ teaspoon salt
2 garlic cloves, minced
2 tablespoons olive oil

DIRECTIONS:

- Set the Pressure cooker on sauté mode and fry garlic for a minute.
- Add oil and SAUTÉ mushrooms for 4-5 minutes.
- Stir in the cream, chicken broth, and cream cheese and season with salt and pepper.
- Cook for 20-25 minutes on MANUAL mode.

Black Lentils Tacos

(Time: 35 minutes \ Servings: 4)

INGREDIENTS:

1 cup black lentils, soaked
½ cup sour cream
2 tomatoes, chopped
¼ cup corn kernels
½ teaspoon chili powder
2-3 garlic cloves, minced

½ teaspoon salt
2 cups water
4 tablespoons cooking oil
¼ cup spinach, chopped
3 tablespoons lemon juice
3-4 corn tortillas

DIRECTIONS:

- Set the Pressure cooker on BEANS mode.
- Add all the ingredients except the tortillas.
- Cook for 20 minutes.
- Place 1-2 tablespoons of the mixture on each tortilla.
- Repeat for all tortillas.
- Drizzle with lemon juice.

Stir Fried Garlic Zest Spinach

(Time: 25 minutes \ Servings: 3)

INGREDIENTS:

2 cups baby spinach
3-4 garlic cloves, thinly sliced
¼ teaspoon salt

½ cup chicken stock
4 tablespoons butter

DIRECTIONS:

- Set the Pressure cooker on SAUTÉ mode, melt the butter and fry the garlic for 20 seconds.
- Add the spinach and stir-fry for 10 minutes.
- Add in the chicken stock and mix well.
- When the water is dried out, season with salt and pepper.

Sweet Potato Casserole

(Time: 45 minutes \ Servings: 4)

INGREDIENTS:

4-5 sweet potatoes, boiled
½ teaspoon ginger powder
½ cup brown sugar
1 pinch salt

½ cup milk
3 eggs
4 tablespoons butter, melted

DIRECTIONS:

- Transfer the boiled sweet potatoes, salt, milk, brown sugar, and ginger powder and blend until smooth.
- Crack the eggs in a blender and blend for another minute.
- Grease the Pressure cooker with butter and transfer the sweet potatoes mixture.
- Cover with a lid and cook for 40-45 minutes on SLOW COOK mode.

Creamy Spinach Pulverize

(Time: 25 minutes \ Servings: 3)

INGREDIENTS:

3 cups spinach, chopped
1 cup heavy cream
¼ teaspoon salt
1 teaspoon black pepper

1 onion, chopped
4-5 garlic cloves, minced
1 cup chicken stock
2 tablespoons butter

DIRECTIONS:

- In the Pressure cooker, melt butter on sauté mode.
- Then sauté onion and garlic for 1 minute.
- Add the spinach and simmer until lightly softened.
- Add in the chicken stock, salt, pepper, and cream and mix well.
- Transfer this mixture to a blender and blend to a puree.
- Pour the blended spinach back into the Pressure cooker and cook for 15 minutes on MANUAL mode.
- Serve hot and enjoy.

Hot Stir-Fried Chili Pepper

(Time: 20 minutes \ Servings: 3)

INGREDIENTS:

2 green bell peppers, sliced
2 red bell peppers, fried
1 onion, sliced
½ teaspoon salt

½ teaspoon chili powder
½ teaspoon garlic paste
2 tablespoons olive oil

DIRECTIONS:

- In the Pressure cooker, heat oil and fry the onion and the garlic.
- Add the salt, chili powder, and bell peppers and keep stirring.
- Stir fry for 10-15 minutes with few splashes of water.
- Transfer to a serving dish and serve.

Creamy Mashed Potatoes Simmer

(Time: 45 minutes \ Servings: 4)

INGREDIENTS:

4 potatoes, boiled, peeled
1 cup milk
¼ lb. mozzarella cheese
¼ teaspoon salt

1 teaspoon black pepper
½ cup parmesan cheese, shredded
2 garlic cloves, minced
2 tablespoons butter

DIRECTIONS:

- Set the Pressure cooker on sauté mode.
- Add butter, onion, and garlic and sauté for 1-2 minute.
- In a bowl, add the potatoes, parmesan cheese, cream, mozzarella cheese, salt, and black pepper, and mash using a potato masher.
- Transfer this mixture to the Pressure cooker and cover with a lid.
- Cook on SLOW COOK mode for 30-40 minutes.

Fried Potatoes

(Time: 35 minutes \ Servings: 3)

INGREDIENTS:

4 potatoes, peeled, thinly sliced
½ teaspoon chili flakes
¼ teaspoon salt

¼ teaspoon turmeric powder
2 tablespoons olive oil

DIRECTIONS:

- Set the Pressure cooker on sauté mode.
- Add the potatoes and cook for 5-10 minutes.
- Season with turmeric, salt and chili flakes.
- Cook on BEANS mode for 10-15 minutes.
- Transfer to a serving dish and enjoy.

Stir Fried Garlic Mushroom

(Time: 35 minutes \ Servings: 4)

INGREDIENTS:

2 cups mushrooms, sliced
2 tablespoons soya sauce
2 tablespoons oyster sauce
¼ teaspoon garlic paste
¼ teaspoon salt
1 cup baby corns

½ teaspoons black pepper
2 tablespoons coconut oil
2 tablespoons cilantro, chopped
¼ cup chicken broth

DIRECTIONS:

- Set the Pressure cooker on sauté mode.
- Heat oil and fry the garlic and the mushrooms for 10 minutes.
- Season with broth, corns, oyster sauce, soya sauce, salt and pepper.
- Cook for 20 minutes on BEANS mode.
- Sprinkle cilantro on top.

Spiced Zucchini Fingers

(Time: 15 minutes \ Servings: 5)

INGREDIENTS:

2 large zucchinis, sliced
1 teaspoon cumin powder
1 teaspoon cinnamon power
¼ teaspoon garlic powder

¼ teaspoon salt
2 tablespoons all-purpose flour
½ teaspoon chili powder
½ cup cooking oil

DIRECTIONS:

- Roll out the zucchini slices into the flour and set aside.
- Set the Pressure cooker on SAUTÉ mode.
- Heat oil and deep fry the zucchinis until lightly golden.
- Drain out the excessive oil on a piece of paper.
- Sprinkle with salt, chili powder, cinnamon powder, and cumin powder.

Thyme Zest Potato Mash

(Time: 35 minutes \ Servings: 5)

INGREDIENTS:

4 baking potatoes
1 teaspoon salt
1 teaspoon black pepper

1 teaspoon garlic paste/powder
4 tablespoons olive oil
3 sprigs of fresh thyme

DIRECTIONS:

- Peel and wash the potatoes. Prick with a fork.
- Drizzle a few drops of oil on the potatoes and place in the Pressure cooker.
- Cook for 20 minutes on MANUAL mode. Sprinkle the potatoes with the spices.

Asparagus Chowder

(Time: 45 minutes \ Servings: 5)

INGREDIENTS:

1 tablespoon olive oil
2 cups chopped onion

2 teaspoons grated lemon rind
1 cup boiled rice

3 cans fat-free, chicken broth
2 cups sliced asparagus
2 cups chopped spinach

¼ teaspoon ground nutmeg
½ cup grated Parmesan cheese
½ teaspoon salt

DIRECTIONS:

- Heat oil in the Pressure cooker.
- Add onion, stirring for 5 minutes until transparent.
- Now add the rice, lemon rind, asparagus, spinach, chicken broth, salt and cook for 10 minutes with covered lid on BEANS mode. Turn off the heat and then top with parmesan cheese and ground nutmeg.

Slow-Cooked Cabbage

(Time: 45 minutes \ Servings: 5)

INGREDIENTS:

4-5 baby cabbages, halved
1 teaspoon salt
1 cup tomato sauce

2 tablespoons olive oil
¼ teaspoon white pepper
½ teaspoon salt

DIRECTIONS:

- Add all ingredients to the Pressure cooker.
- Cook on SLOW COOK mode for 45 minutes.

Eggplant and Tomato Curry

(Time: 25 minutes \ Servings: 4)

INGREDIENTS:

3 eggplants, cut into small pieces
1 onion, chopped
3 large tomatoes, chopped
½ teaspoon salt
1 teaspoon chili powder

¼ teaspoon turmeric powder
½ teaspoon garlic paste
½ teaspoon ginger paste
¼ cup cooking oil

DIRECTIONS:

- Heat oil in the Pressure cooker on SAUTÉ mode.
- Add the eggplants and fry until golden, then set aside.
- In the same oil, sauté onion until transparent.
- Add in the tomatoes, salt, chili powder, turmeric powder, ginger paste, garlic paste and fry well.
- Add the fried eggplants and cook for 10-14 minutes on EGG setting.

Chili and Garlic Zest Pumpkin

(Time: 30 minutes \ Servings: 3)

INGREDIENTS:

2 cups pumpkin, cut into small slices
3 green chilies, chopped
¼ teaspoon salt
1 teaspoon chili powder

¼ teaspoon turmeric powder
½ teaspoon garlic paste
2 tablespoons cooking oil

DIRECTIONS:

- Heat oil in the Pressure cooker on SAUTÉ mode and fry the garlic and the green chilies for a minute.
- Add in the salt, chili powder, turmeric powder and the pumpkin slices and cook on MANUAL for 10-15 minutes. Then cover with a lid and cook on MANUAL for another 10 minutes.

Peas and Carrots with Potatoes

(Time: 40 minutes \ Servings: 5)

INGREDIENTS:

1 cup peas
1 cup cauliflower florets
3 potatoes, small cubes
2 carrots, peeled, cut into small cubes
1 onion, chopped
1 teaspoon salt
1 teaspoon chili powder
¼ teaspoon turmeric powder

½ teaspoon cumin powder
2 tomatoes chopped
½ teaspoon cinnamon powder
½ teaspoon garlic paste
2 tablespoons cooking oil
1 cup water
3 cups of boiled rice

DIRECTIONS:

- Heat oil in the Pressure cooker on SAUTÉ mode and sauté onion until transparent.
- Add in the tomatoes, salt, chili powder, turmeric powder, ginger paste, garlic paste and keep frying. Add all vegetables and fry for 10-15 minutes. Add the water and cover with a lid. Let simmer for 15 minutes. Serve with boiled rice.

Slow Cooked Honey Glazed Carrots

(Time: 45 minutes \ Servings: 5)

INGREDIENTS:

1 oz. carrots, peeled
1 tablespoon red wine vinegar
2 tablespoons of unsalted butter
1 teaspoon black pepper

1 pinch salt
1 cup water
½ cup brown sugar
2 tablespoons honey

DIRECTIONS:

- Add all ingredients in the Pressure cooker except the honey.
- Cook on SLOW COOK mode for 45 minutes.
- Drizzle honey on top and serve.

Tropic Cauliflower Manchurian

(Time: 35 minutes \ Servings: 4)

INGREDIENTS:

2 cups cauliflower florets
1 onion, chopped
1 teaspoon salt
1 teaspoon chili flakes
½ teaspoon cumin powder
3 green chilies, sliced

1 cup tomato puree
3 tablespoons tomato ketchup
½ teaspoon cinnamon powder
½ teaspoon garlic paste
¼ teaspoon turmeric powder
¼ cup cooking oil

DIRECTIONS:

- Heat oil in the Pressure cooker on SAUTÉ mode.
- Add the cauliflower florets and fry until lightly golden, then set aside.
- In the same pot, sauté onion until transparent.
- Add in the tomato puree, tomato ketchup, salt, chili flakes, turmeric powder, and garlic paste and fry for 5-6 minutes.
- Add in the cauliflower and fry again for 4-5 minutes.
- Sprinkle cinnamon powder, cumin powder, and green chilies on top.

Garlic Fried Mushrooms

(Time: 15 minutes \ Servings: 3)

INGREDIENTS:

2 cups mushrooms, sliced
¼ teaspoon salt
1 teaspoon black pepper
½ teaspoon garlic paste

2 tablespoons soya sauce
1 teaspoon basil, chopped
2 tablespoons cooking oil

DIRECTIONS:

- Heat oil on SAUTÉ mode.
- Fry garlic for 30 seconds.
- Stir in the mushrooms and stir-fry for 5-10 minutes on.
- Add in the soya sauce and season with salt and pepper.
- Cook for 5 more minutes, stirring occasionally.
- Sprinkle basil on top and serve.

Rice with Carrots

(Time: 35 minutes \ Servings: 4)

INGREDIENTS:

2 cups rice, soaked
2 carrots, peeled, chopped
1 potato, peeled, chopped
1 teaspoon cumin seeds
1 black cardamom
2-3 cinnamon sticks

1 tomato, sliced
2 large onions, sliced
1 teaspoon salt
4 tablespoons olive oil
4 cups vegetables broth

DIRECTIONS:

- Heat oil on SAUTÉ mode.
- Cook the onion, cumin seeds, cinnamon sticks and cardamom, until golden.
- Add the carrots, potatoes, salt, and chili powder and fry.
- Then add the tomato slices and pour in the vegetable broth, then press RICE mode.
- Add the rice and when bubbles appear on the top, cover the pot.
- Cook for 20 minutes.

Tropic Potato Gravy

(Time: 25 minutes \ Servings: 4)

INGREDIENTS:

4 potatoes, boiled, peeled, cut into
    cubes
1 onion, chopped
1 teaspoon cumin seeds
1 teaspoon chili powder
½ teaspoon cumin powder
1 cup tomato puree

½ teaspoon cinnamon powder
½ teaspoon garlic paste
½ teaspoon thyme
¼ teaspoon turmeric powder
2 tablespoons cooking oil
½ cup chicken broth

DIRECTIONS:

- Heat oil in the Pressure cooker on SAUTÉ mode and sauté onion, cumin seeds and garlic for 1 minute.
- Add in the tomato puree, salt, chili powder, turmeric powder, and garlic paste and fry for 5-6 minutes.
- Add the potatoes and mix thoroughly.
- Stir in the chicken broth and cook for 10 minutes on BROTH mode.
- Sprinkle cinnamon powder, thyme and cumin powder on top.

Ground Beef Zucchini Zoodles

(Time: 35 minutes \ Servings: 4)

INGREDIENTS:

¼ lb. beef mince
1 large zucchini, spiralled
1 onion, chopped
2 tablespoons olive oil
2 tomatoes, chopped
2-3 garlic cloves, minced

½ teaspoon black pepper
¼ teaspoon chili powder
2 tablespoons soya sauce
1 oz. parmesan cheese, grated
¼ teaspoon salt

DIRECTIONS:

- Heat oil on SAUTÉ mode. Fry onion and garlic for a minute.
- Add the beef and fry until brown.
- Add in the tomatoes, salt, chili powder, soya sauce and black pepper.
- Transfer the fried ground beef to a bowl and set aside.
- In the same pot, add the zucchini zoodles and fry for 5-10 minutes.
- Add in the fried ground beef and mix well. Sprinkle cheese on top.

Spinach Black Beans Chili

(Time: 45 minutes \ Servings: 4)

INGREDIENTS:

2 cans of black beans
2 tomatoes, chopped
1 cup spinach, chopped
1 cup red bell pepper, chopped
2 large onions, chopped
1 teaspoon salt
3 garlic cloves, minced

2 tablespoons olive oil
4 cups vegetables broth
½ teaspoon black pepper
1 teaspoon red chili powder
1 bunch coriander, chopped
2 tablespoons sour cream
2 green chilies, chopped

DIRECTIONS:

- In the Pressure cooker, add all ingredients, stir well and cover with a lid.
- Cook on SLOW COOK mode for 40-45 minutes.
- Transfer to a serving dish and sprinkle coriander. Top with sour cream.

Sweet Potato Mash with Oregano

(Time: 35 minutes \ Servings: 5)

INGREDIENTS:

4 sweet potatoes
1 teaspoon salt
1 teaspoon black pepper

1 teaspoon garlic paste/powder
4 tablespoons olive oil
2 tablespoons oregano

DIRECTIONS:

- Peel and wash the potatoes. Prick with a fork.
- Drizzle a few drops of oil on the potatoes and place in the Pressure cooker.
- Cook for 20-25 minutes on MANUAL mode.
- Sprinkle the potatoes with the spices.

Mashed Potato Pilaf

(Time: 45 minutes \ Servings: 5)

INGREDIENTS:

2 cups rice, soaked
3 potatoes, boiled, mashed
1 teaspoon cumin seeds
1 carrot, peeled, chopped
1 bay leaf
2 garlic cloves, minced

2 cloves
1 tomato, chopped
2 large onions, sliced
1 teaspoon salt
4 tablespoons olive oil
4 cups vegetables broth

DIRECTIONS:

- Heat oil in the Pressure cooker on SAUTÉ mode.
- Fry onion and the cumin seeds, bay leaf and cloves until brown.
- Add in the potatoes, carrots, salt, chili powder, and garlic and fry.
- Add in the tomatoes and stir fry until the potatoes are softened.
- Pour in vegetable broth and boil.
- Add the rice and cover the pot when bubbles appear on the surface.
- Cook for 20 minutes on RICE mode.

Eggplant and Potato Gravy

(Time: 55 minutes \ Servings: 5)

INGREDIENTS:

2 eggplants, sliced
2 potatoes, peeled, diced
1 onion, chopped
3 large tomatoes, chopped
½ teaspoon salt

1 teaspoon chili powder
¼ teaspoon dry coriander powder
¼ teaspoon turmeric powder
½ teaspoon garlic paste
2 tablespoons cooking oil

DIRECTIONS:

- Heat oil in the Pressure cooker on SAUTÉ mode and sauté onion until transparent.
- Add in the tomatoes, salt, chili powder, turmeric powder, and garlic paste and fry well.
- Add the eggplants and fry for 15 minutes on high heat.
- Add the potatoes, stirring continuously.

- Add a few splashes of water while frying.
- Cover with a lid and cook on MANUAL for 10 minutes.
- Sprinkle cumin powder and mix thoroughly.

Cabbage with Potatoes

(Time: 35 minutes \ Servings: 5)

INGREDIENTS:

1 cup cabbage, chopped
2 potatoes, sliced
1 onion, chopped
2 tomatoes, chopped
½ teaspoon salt

1 teaspoon chili powder
¼ teaspoon turmeric powder
½ teaspoon garlic paste
2-3 green chilies, chopped
2 tablespoons cooking oil

DIRECTIONS:

- Heat oil in the Pressure cooker on SAUTÉ mode, sauté onion until transparent.
- Add in the tomatoes, salt, chili powder, turmeric powder, and garlic paste and fry for 5-10 minutes.
- Add the cabbage and fry well.
- Add the potatoes and stir well until the potatoes are softened.
- Cook on MANUAL for 10 minutes.

Cheese Omelette

(Time: 15 minutes \ Servings: 2)

INGREDIENTS:

2 eggs, whisked
1 teaspoon garlic powder
¼ teaspoons slat
½ teaspoon black pepper

½ cup parmesan cheese, shredded
½ cup mozzarella cheese, shredded
3 tablespoons butter

DIRECTIONS:

- In a bowl, add the eggs, mozzarella and parmesan cheese, season with salt, garlic and pepper.
- Melt butter in the Pressure cooker on SAUTÉ mode.
- Pour the eggs' mixture and spread evenly all over.
- Cook for 2-3 minutes from one each side.
- Serve hot and enjoy.

Egg Scramble

(Time: 10 minutes \ Servings: 3)

INGREDIENTS:

4 eggs
1 pinch of salt
½ teaspoon black pepper

1 cup milk
3 tablespoons butter

DIRECTIONS:

- Melt butter in the pot on SAUTÉ mode. Crack the eggs and add milk, stir continuously for 5 minutes.
- Transfer to a serving platter and scramble again with a fork.

Egg and Onion Frittata

(Time: 25 minutes \ Servings: 3)

INGREDIENTS:

4 eggs, whisked
1 onion, chopped
1 green chili, chopped

¼ teaspoons slat
½ teaspoon black pepper
3 tablespoons butter

DIRECTIONS:

- In a bowl, add eggs, onion, green chilies, salt, and pepper, mix well.
- Melt butter in the Pressure cooker on SAUTÉ mode.
- Transfer the eggs mixture and spread all over.
- Cook for 2-3 minutes from on each side.

Egg and Carrots Crumb

(Time: 25 minutes \ Servings: 3)

INGREDIENTS:

4 eggs
1 carrot, shredded
1 pinch of salt

½ teaspoon black pepper
3 tablespoons butter

DIRECTIONS:

- Melt butter on SAUTÉ mode.
- Sauté carrots for 5-10 minutes until the water evaporates.
- Add the eggs, salt and pepper, stir continuously.
- Cook for 5 minutes.

Half Fry Eggs

(Time: 5 minutes \ Servings: 2)

INGREDIENTS:

2 eggs
1 pinch of salt

½ teaspoon black pepper
3 tablespoons oil

DIRECTIONS:

- Heat oil in the Pressure cooker on SAUTÉ mode.
- Crack eggs in the pot and cook for 2-3 minutes.
- Transfer to a platter and season with salt and pepper.

Bell Pepper and Egg Tortilla

(Time: 25 minutes \ Servings: 3)

INGREDIENTS:

4 eggs, whisked
1 red bell pepper, chopped
1 onion, chopped

¼ teaspoons slat
½ teaspoon black pepper
3 tablespoons butter

DIRECTIONS:

- In a bowl, add the eggs, onion, bell peppers, salt, and pepper, mix well.
- Melt butter in the pot on SAUTÉ mode.
- Pour the eggs mixture and spread all over and cover the pot with a lid.
- Cook for 15 minutes on MANUAL mode.
- Serve hot and enjoy.

Hard Boiled Eggs

(Time: 20 minutes \ Servings: 4)

INGREDIENTS:

4 eggs
2 tablespoons salt

3 cups water

DIRECTIONS:

- Fill the Pressure cooker with water and add salt.
- Place the eggs in the water and cover up with a lid.
- Let them boil on EGG mode for 10 minutes.
- Remove from the pot and transfer to cold water.

Avocado eggs

(Time: 20 minutes \ Servings: 2)

INGREDIENTS:

2 eggs
1 avocado, pitted, halved
1 pinch salt

1 pinch black pepper
2 tablespoons olive oil

DIRECTIONS:

- Spray the Pressure cooker with oil. Place the avocados in the Pressure cooker and crack the eggs into each avocado half.
- Season with salt and pepper.
- Cover and cook for 15 minutes on MANUAL mode.

Roasted Eggs Gravy

(Time: 30 minutes \ Servings: 4)

INGREDIENTS:

4 eggs
1 onion, chopped
2 tomatoes, chopped
¼ teaspoon pinch salt
½ teaspoon chili powder

¼ teaspoon turmeric powder
1/3 teaspoon cumin powder
1 garlic cloves, minced
2 tablespoons olive oil

DIRECTIONS:

- Heat oil in the Pressure cooker on SAUTÉ mode and fry the eggs until lightly golden. Set aside.
- In the same oil, fry onion until lightly golden.
- Add tomatoes, garlic, salt, chili powder, and turmeric powder and fry until the tomatoes soften.
- Now transfer to a blender and blend well.
- Return the mixture to the pot again and fry with a few splashes of water.
- Add in the roasted eggs and toss around.

Squash with Eggs

(Time: 30 minutes \ Servings: 4)

INGREDIENTS:

4 eggs
1 squash, cut into 1-inch thick rings
1 pinch salt
1 pinch chili powder

2 tablespoons olive oil

DIRECTIONS:
- Spray the Pressure cooker with oil.
- Place the squash rings in the Pressure cooker and crack an egg into each ring.
- Sprinkle with salt and pepper. Cover with a lid and cook for 25 minutes on MANUAL mode.

Pepper Egg

(Time: 5 minutes \ Servings: 1)

INGREDIENTS:

1 egg
1 large yellow bell pepper sliced
1 pinch salt

1 pinch black pepper
2 tablespoons olive oil

DIRECTIONS:
- Spray the Pressure cooker with oil.
- Place the bell pepper in the Pressure cooker and crack the egg in the center.
- Season with salt and pepper.
- Cover with a lid and cook for 5 minutes on EGG mode.

Tomato Eggs

(Time: 10 minutes \ Servings: 2)

INGREDIENTS:

2 eggs, whisked
2 tomatoes, sliced
1 teaspoon garlic powder

¼ teaspoon salt
½ teaspoon chili powder
3 tablespoons butter

DIRECTIONS:
- Melt butter on SAUTÉ mode. Add the eggs and spread all over. Cook for 1-2 minutes then flip.
- Place the tomato slices and in the Pressure cooker and cover the pot with a lid.
- Cook on MANUAL mode for 10 minutes. Season with salt and chili powder.

Zucchini Egg

(Time: 15 minutes \ Servings: 2)

INGREDIENTS:

2 eggs, whisked
1 large zucchini, sliced
1 teaspoon garlic powder

¼ teaspoon salt
¼ teaspoon black pepper
3 tablespoons butter

DIRECTIONS:

- Melt butter in the Pressure cooker on SAUTÉ mode. Fry zucchini for 3-4 minutes.
- Pour the eggs mixture and spread evenly. Cook for 2-3 minutes on one side then flip over.
- Season with salt and pepper.

Egg Mac

(Time: 25 minutes \ Servings: 2)

INGREDIENTS:

2 eggs, whisked
1 teaspoon garlic powder
¼ teaspoons slat
½ teaspoon black pepper

1 onion chopped
1 cup macaroni, boiled
1 tomato, chopped
3 tablespoons oil

DIRECTIONS:

- Combine the eggs with the macaroni, onion, salt, pepper, and garlic powder, mix well.
- Heat oil in the Pressure cooker on SAUTÉ mode.
- Pour the eggs mixture and stir.
- Cook for 1-2 minutes.

Poached Eggs

(Time: 10 minutes \ Servings: 3)

INGREDIENTS:

3 eggs
3 cups water

2 tablespoons vinegar
1 pinch salt

DIRECTIONS:

- Set the Pressure cooker on MANUAL mode. Add water and let it boil.
- Crack 1 egg into a bowl and pour it in the boiled water. Repeat for all eggs. Cover with a lid and cook for 5 minutes. Ladle to a serving platter and enjoy.

Coated Eggs

(Time: 45 minutes \ Servings: 4)

INGREDIENTS:

4 hardboiled eggs, peeled
1 teaspoon garlic powder
¼ teaspoon salt
½ teaspoon black pepper

1 cup chicken mince
2 tablespoons gram flour
1 cup oil, for frying

DIRECTIONS:

- Combine the gram flour, mince, garlic powder, salt and pepper, mix well. Take 2-3 tablespoons of this mixture and coat in an egg. Repeat for all eggs.
- Heat oil in the Pressure cooker on SAUTÉ mode. Fry the eggs until golden. Place to a paper towel.

Spinach Egg Frittata

(Time: 25 minutes \ Servings: 2)

INGREDIENTS:

2 eggs, whisked
1 cup spinach, chopped
1 cup cherry tomatoes, sliced

¼ teaspoons salt
½ teaspoon black pepper
3 tablespoons butter

DIRECTIONS:

- Add the spinach and tomatoes.
- Season with salt, garlic and pepper.
- Melt butter in the Pressure cooker on SAUTÉ mode.
- Pour the eggs mixture and spread all over.
- Cook each side for 4 minutes.

Asian Style Steamed Eggs

(Time: 10 Minutes \ Servings: 2)

INGREDIENTS

2 large eggs
⅓ cup of cold water
2 stem of scallions, chopped
1 pinch of sesame seeds
1 pinch of fine garlic powder
pinch of salt and black pepper

1 pinch of flax seeds powder
2 avocados
1 tsp. of ginger
1 tsp. of flax seed powder
1 tbsp. of coconut oil

DIRECTIONS

- Start by placing the eggs into the water in a small bowl.
- Strain the eggs mixture above a mesh strainer above a heat proof bowl.
- Now, add what is left of the ingredients, except for the avocados.
- Mix very well and set aside. Pour water in the inner pot of the Pressure cooker and place the trivet or the steamer basket. Place the bowl with the above mixture inside the trivet or the steamer basket.
- Seal the lid of the Pressure cooker tightly and make sure to close the vent valve. Now, press MANUAL and cook for 5 minutes. And when you hear the beep, open the lid and serve the eggs with cooked quinoa and the avocado.

Eggs Steamed in Avocado

(Time: 10 Minutes \ Servings: 4)

INGREDIENTS

2 avocados, ripened
4 large eggs
¼ tsp. of black pepper

¼ tsp. of ground ginger
1 tbsp. of chopped chives

DIRECTIONS

- Halve the avocados and take the pit out. Scoop two tablespoons from its center so enough space is created for the eggs.
- Pour a cup of water inside the Pressure cooker and place a trivet or a steamer basket inside.
- Line the avocados into the steamer basket and crack each egg into each avocado half; then let the white spill into the avocado gradually.
- Repeat the same procedure with the rest of the avocado halves. Close the lid tightly and seal the vent valve.
- Press the button MANUAL for 10 minutes.
- Once the timer goes off, release the pressure. Season the eggs with, salt, pepper, ginger, and chives.

Soups and Stews

Pumpkin and Potato Soup

(Time: 35 minutes \ Servings: 4)

INGREDIENTS:

1 cup pumpkin chunks, peeled
2 potatoes, cut into small cubes
2 cups vegetable broth
1 cup milk
2 tablespoons fish sauce

¼ teaspoon turmeric powder
½ teaspoon chili powder
4-5 garlic cloves, minced
¼ teaspoon salt
1 tablespoon oil

DIRECTIONS:

- Heat oil in the Pressure cooker on SAUTÉ and add the garlic cloves, cook for 1 minute.
- Add the pumpkin and the potatoes and cook for 5 minutes.
- Stir in the vegetable broth, salt, chili powder, turmeric powder, and fish sauce and mix.
- Cook on SOUP mode for 20 minutes. Add the milk and cook for another 5 minutes.
- Turn off the heat and ladle the soup into serving bowls.

Mushroom Soup

(Time: 35 minutes \ Servings: 3)

INGREDIENTS:

1 cup mushrooms, sliced
1 onion, sliced
1 cup chicken broth
3 garlic cloves, minced

¼ teaspoon ginger paste
½ teaspoon black pepper
¼ teaspoon salt
1 tablespoon oil

DIRECTIONS:

- Heat oil in the Pressure cooker, add onion and garlic cloves, sauté for 1 minute on SAUTÉ mode.
- Add the mushrooms with ginger paste and stir fry for 5 minutes.
- Pour in the chicken broth, salt, and pepper and mix well.
- Cook on SOUP for 25 minutes. Pour to serving bowls.

Cauliflower Soup

(Time: 35 minutes \ Servings: 4)

INGREDIENTS:

1 cup cauliflower florets
1 teaspoon ginger paste
1 red bell pepper chopped
2 cups vegetable broth
2 tablespoons vinegar
1 lemon, sliced

1 green chili, chopped
4-5 garlic cloves, minced
½ teaspoon black pepper
¼ teaspoon salt
1 tablespoon oil

DIRECTIONS:

- Heat oil in the Pressure cooker, add the ginger paste and cook for 1 minute on SAUTÉ mode.
- Add the cauliflower and fry well for 5-10 minutes.
- Add the bell pepper, salt, pepper, vinegar, green chilies, and lemon slices and mix well.
- Add the vegetable broth and cook on SOUP for 15 minutes.
- Pour into serving bowls.

Peas and Spinach Soup

(Time: 15 minutes \ Servings: 4)

INGREDIENTS:

1 cup baby spinach
1 cup peas
2 cups vegetable broth
½ cup milk
4-5 garlic cloves, minced

1 cup cream
½ cup tofu
½ teaspoon chili flakes
¼ teaspoon salt
2 tablespoons oil

DIRECTIONS:

- Heat oil in the saucepan and add the garlic cloves, cook for 1 minute on SAUTÉ mode.
- Add the vegetable broth, spinach, peas, tofu, cream, chili flake and salt, mix well.
- Cook on SOUP mode for 10 minutes. Perform a quick pressure release.
- Pour in the milk and cook for another 5 minutes on SOUP mode.
- Serve in bowls.

Shrimp Soup

(Time: 25 minutes \ Servings: 4)

INGREDIENTS:

2 oz. shrimp
2 cups chicken broth
¼ cup apple cider vinegar
4-5 garlic cloves, minced

½ teaspoon black pepper
¼ teaspoon salt
1 tablespoon oil
2 tomatoes, sliced

DIRECTIONS:

- Heat oil and add garlic cloves, fry for 1 minute. Add the shrimp and fry for 10 minutes.
- Season with salt and pepper.
- Add chicken broth, tomatoes, and vinegar and stir well.
- Cook on SOUP mode for 15 minutes.
- Pour into serving bowls.

Chicken Corn Soup

(Time: 25 minutes \ Servings: 3)

INGREDIENTS:

1 cup chicken, boiled, shredded
¼ cup water
2 tablespoons corn flour
3 cups chicken broth

1 garlic clove minced
¼ teaspoon salt
¼ teaspoon black pepper
2 tablespoons cooking oil

DIRECTIONS:

- Heat oil in the Pressure cooker and fry garlic for 30 seconds.
- Add shredded chicken and stir fry.
- Add chicken broth and cook for 20 minutes on SOUP mode.
- Combine the corn flour with water and pour gradually into the soup until it thickens.
- Season the soup with salt and pepper. Ladle to a serving dish and serve.

Chickpea and Basil Soup

(Time: 35 minutes \ Servings: 3)

INGREDIENTS:

1 cup chickpeas, boiled
2-3 basil leaves
3 cups vegetable broth
1 garlic clove minced

¼ teaspoon salt
¼ teaspoon chili powder
¼ teaspoon black pepper
2 tablespoons cooking oil

DIRECTIONS:

- In the Pressure cooker, add all ingredients and cook on SOUP mode for 30 minutes.
- Transfer to serving bowls and serve hot.

Chicken and Mushroom Soup

(Time: 15 minutes \ Servings: 2)

INGREDIENTS:

¼ cup oil
¼ cup all-purpose flour
1 bell pepper, sliced
1 onion , chopped
2 cups chicken breast, chopped
4 oz. mushrooms

2 tomatoes , diced
3 garlic cloves
1 tsp. soy sauce
1 tsp. sugar
salt and pepper, to taste
3 drops hot sauce

DIRECTIONS:

- Add oil into the pressure cooker and let it sauté.
- Mix bell pepper, chicken, mushrooms, tomatoes, onion, soy sauce, garlic, sugar and hot sauce. Add salt and pepper.
- Add flour and stir well. Let it cook on SOUP mode for 10 minutes.

Turkey Mixed Soup Recipe

(Time: 20 minutes \ Servings: 2)

INGREDIENTS:

3 cups turkey, cubed
2 cups water
3 stalks celery, chopped
2 garlic cloves

2 onions, chopped
salt and pepper, to taste
2 cups green onion chopped

DIRECTIONS:

- Add water and turkey cubes into the pressure cooker.
- Add celery, garlic, salt and pepper, onion and green onion. Stir well.
- Cook it on SOUP mode for 15 minutes and serve hot.

Cheesy Chicken Recipe

(Time: 16 minutes \ Servings: 2)

INGREDIENTS:

1 tbsp. sour cream
1 tbsp. ranch dressing
4 bacon slices

1 lb. chicken breast, cubed
1 cup cheddar cheese
3 cups chicken broth

DIRECTIONS:

- Mix sour cream, ranch dressing, bacon slices, chicken and cheddar cheese in a bowl.
- Add the mixture into the pressure cooker. Cook for 10 minutes on POULTRY mode.
- Mix in the chicken broth and cook for 4 more minutes.

Chicken and Green Onion Soup

(Time: 14 minutes \ Servings: 3)

INGREDIENTS:

1 lb. chicken breast, shredded
2 cups chicken stock
1 tbsp. ginger

2 tbsp. sesame oil
salt to taste
green onions, chopped

DIRECTIONS:

- Add sesame oil into the pressure cooker and SAUTÉ it.
- Mix in the chicken stock, chicken breast, ginger, salt and green onions.
- Cook on SOUP mode for 10 minutes.

Vegetable Broth with Veggies Soup

(Time: 20 minutes \ Servings: 3)

INGREDIENTS:

2 tbsp. olive oil
1 onion, chopped
2 cups vegetable broth
3 potatoes, diced

1 tsp. thyme
2 tbsp. apple cider vinegar
2 carrots, sliced
parsley to garnish

DIRECTIONS:

- Add oil into the pressure cooker and SAUTÉ it.
- Mix in the vegetable broth, thyme, apple cider vinegar, carrots, potatoes and onion.
- Cook for 14 minutes on SOUP mode.
- When done, garnish with chopped parsley and serve.

Black Beans Mix Soup

(Time: 16 minutes \ Servings: 2)

INGREDIENTS:

4 cups black beans
3 onions , chopped
2 tbsp. olive oil
1 tbsp. oregano

1 tbsp. chili powder
½ cup green chilies
cilantro leaves to garnish
salt to taste

DIRECTIONS:

- Add oil into the pressure cooker and SAUTÉ it.
- Mix in the onions, salt, oregano, green chilies, chili powder and black beans.
- Cook on SOUP mode for 10 minutes.
- When done, serve and enjoy the meal.

Corn and Potato Mix Soup

(Time: 15 minutes \ Servings: 3)

INGREDIENTS:

1 tbsp. butter
2 cups chicken broth
2 tbsp. cornstarch
2 tbsp. red pepper flakes

1 onion , chopped
2 potatoes, cubed
1 cup corn

4 slices bacon, chopped, cooked

DIRECTIONS:

- Add butter into the pressure cooker and let it sauté.
- Mix in the chicken broth with cornstarch, red pepper flakes, onion, potatoes, corn and bacon. Cook for 15 minutes on SOUP mode.

Delicious Full Chicken Soup

(Time: 13 minutes \ Servings: 2)

INGREDIENTS:

2 lb. chicken breast fillet, strips
1 tbsp. canola oil
1 tsp. oregano powder
2 red bell peppers, sliced
2 green bell peppers, sliced

2 onions, sliced
4 slices provolone cheese
4 cups chicken broth
salt and pepper, to taste

DIRECTIONS:

- Add canola oil into the pressure cooker and cook chicken fillets.
- Mix in the oregano powder, salt and pepper, red bell pepper, green bell pepper and onion. Cook for 10 minutes on SAUTÉ mode.
- Add chicken broth.
- Cook for 10 minutes on SOUP mode.
- When done, serve and enjoy!

Chicken Noodle Soup

(Time: 15 minutes \ Servings: 3)

INGREDIENTS:

1 lb. chicken breast, cubed
1 small package of noodles
1 lb. Bok Choy
4 cups chicken stock

2 cups hot water
2 carrots
salt to taste

DIRECTIONS:

- Add chicken stock into the pressure cooker. Cook for 5 minutes on SOUP mode.
- Mix chicken, Bok Choy, carrots, noodles, salt and hot water into the cooker.
- Cook on SOUP mode for 10 minutes.
- When the pot beeps, release the pressure and enjoy!

Beef Soup

(Time: 14 minutes \ Servings: 3)

INGREDIENTS:

1 lb. ground beef
1 onion , diced
2 garlic cloves , minced
2 cups beans, any
1 potato, cubed

2 tomatoes, cubed
2 celery stalks, chopped
2 tbsp. cumin powder
salt and pepper, to taste

DIRECTIONS:

- Add onion and potato in the pressure cooker. Stir-fry well on SAUTÉ mode.
- Mix in the ground beef, garlic, beans, tomatoes, celery stalks and cumin powder.
- Stir well.
- Cook for 10 minutes in high pressure.
- When done, serve and enjoy!

Sweet Potato Soup

(Time: 16 minutes \ Servings: 2)

INGREDIENTS:

2 tbsp. butter
1 onion
2 sweet potatoes
2 cups corn

2 cups chicken broth
1 tbsp. cornstarch
1 tbsp. red pepper flakes
salt and pepper, to taste

DIRECTIONS:

- Add butter and onion into the pressure cooker. Sauté for 2 minutes.
- Mix chicken broth into it and stir well.
- Add sweet potatoes, corn, salt and pepper, cornstarch and red pepper flakes.
- Cook for 10 minutes on SOUP mode.
- When ready, serve!

Vegetable Soup

(Time: 30 minutes \ Servings: 3)

INGREDIENTS:

1 cup broccoli florets
1 green bell pepper, sliced
1 red bell pepper, sliced
1 carrot, sliced
1 onion, sliced
2 cups vegetable broth

1 tablespoon lemon juice
4-5 garlic cloves, minced
½ teaspoon black pepper
¼ teaspoon salt
1 tablespoon cooking oil

DIRECTIONS:

- Set the Pressure cooker on SAUTÉ mode.
- Heat oil, add onion and garlic cloves, sauté for 1 minute.
- Add all vegetables, stir fry and cook on low heat for 5-10 minutes.
- Add vegetable broth, salt, and pepper and mix well.
- Cook on SOUP mode for 15 minutes.
- Drizzle lemon juice.
- Ladle into serving bowls and enjoy.

Garlic Chicken and Egg Soup

(Time: 35 minutes \ Servings: 3)

INGREDIENTS:

¼ lb. chicken, cut into small pieces
1 onion, chopped
2 eggs, whisked
2 cups chicken broth
¼ cup water

3 tablespoons of flour
4-5 garlic cloves, minced
½ teaspoon black pepper
¼ teaspoon salt
1 tablespoon oil

DIRECTIONS:

- Heat oil in the Pressure cooker on SAUTÉ mode, sauté garlic and onion for 1 minute.
- Add the chicken and fry for 10 minutes.
- Shred chicken and transfer it to the Pressure cooker again.
- Season with black pepper and salt.
- Add the chicken broth, simmer for 15 minutes on SOUP mode.
- In a bowl, combine water with corn flour and mix well.
- Gradually pour this mixture into soup and stir continuously for 2 minutes.
- Add the eggs by gradually. Cook for another 2 minutes. Ladle into bowls.

Pumpkin Purée Soup

(Time: 35 minutes \ Servings: 3)

INGREDIENTS:

2 cups pumpkin puree
2 cups vegetable broth
1 cup milk
2 tablespoons soya sauce
¼ teaspoon turmeric powder

½ teaspoon black pepper
4-5 garlic cloves, minced
¼ teaspoon salt
1 tablespoon oil

DIRECTIONS:

- Heat oil in the Pressure cooker and add garlic cloves, cook for 1 minute on SAUTÉ mode.
- Add pumpkin and fry for 5 minutes.
- Stir in vegetable broth, salt, pepper, turmeric powder, and soya sauce and mix, cook on low heat for 20 minutes on SOUP mode.
- Add milk and cook for another 5 minutes. Ladle the soup into serving bowls.

Spinach Soup

(Time: 35 minutes \ Servings: 3)

INGREDIENTS:

1 cup baby spinach
2 cups vegetable broth
½ cup milk
2 garlic cloves, minced

½ teaspoon chili flakes
¼ teaspoon salt
¼ cup sour cream
2 tablespoons oil

DIRECTIONS:

- In the Pressure cooker, add all ingredients and cover with a lid.
- Set the cooker on SOUP mode, cook for 25 minutes.
- Transfer to a blender and blend until creamy.
- Pour the spinach soup back into the pressure cooker and cook for another 6 minutes.
- Top with sour cream.

Onion and Carrot Soup

(Time: 35 minutes \ Servings: 3)

INGREDIENTS:

1 onion, sliced
2 carrots, chopped
1 tablespoon fish sauce
2 cups chicken broth
1 egg, whisked
2 tablespoons vinegar

1 cup tomato puree
4-5 garlic cloves, minced
½ teaspoon black pepper
¼ teaspoon salt
1 tablespoon oil

DIRECTIONS:

- Heat oil in the Pressure cooker and add garlic cloves and onion, cook for 1 minute on SAUTÉ mode.
- Stir in the carrots and cook for 2 minutes.
- Add soya sauce, salt, pepper, and fish sauce and stir.
- Add chicken broth, and tomato puree and cook for 15 minutes on SOUP mode.
- Add the egg and stir continuously. Ladle into serving bowls.

Yellow Lentils Hot Soup

(Time: 60 minutes \ Servings: 3)

INGREDIENTS:

1 cup yellow lentils, soaked
1 cup water

¼ teaspoon turmeric powder
½ teaspoon ginger paste

1 onion, chopped
3 cups chicken broth
4-5 garlic cloves, minced

½ teaspoon chili powder
¼ teaspoon salt
2 tablespoons butter

DIRECTIONS:

- In the Pressure cooker, add all ingredients and stir.
- Set the pot on slow mode and cover up with a lid.
- Cook for 35 minutes on SOUP mode.
- Pour the soup into bowls and serve.

Red Beans Soup

(Time: 35 minutes \ Servings: 3)

INGREDIENTS:

2 cups red beans, boiled
1 onion, sliced
1 tomato chopped
2 cups chicken broth
1 tablespoon lemon juice

4-5 garlic cloves, minced
½ teaspoon black pepper
¼ teaspoon salt
1 green chili, chopped
1 tablespoon oil

DIRECTIONS:

- Heat oil in the Pressure cooker and sauté garlic with onion for 1 minute on sauté mode.
- Stir in the beans, chicken broth, salt, pepper, and green chili.
- Cook on MANUAL mode for 30 minutes.
- Ladle into serving bowls and drizzle lemon juice.

Potato Cream Soup

(Time: 35 minutes \ Servings: 3)

INGREDIENTS:

4 large potatoes, boiled, mashed
1 onion, sliced
2 cups chicken broth
1 cup heavy cream

3 garlic cloves, minced
½ teaspoon black pepper
¼ teaspoon salt
1 tablespoon oil

DIRECTIONS:

- Heat oil in the Pressure cooker, add onion and garlic cloves, cook for 1 minute on SAUTÉ mode.
- Add the boiled potatoes and stir well.
- Stir in cream, chicken broth, salt, and pepper.
- Cook for 20 minutes on SOUP mode.
- Remove from the heat and let cool a little bit.

- Transfer into a food processor and blend to a puree.
- Pour into the Pressure cooker and cook for 5 minutes.
- Ladle into serving bowls and drizzle lemon juice.

Butter Squash Soup

(Time: 25 Minutes \ Servings: 6)

INGREDIENTS

1 peeled and diced butternut squash.
1 peeled and diced apple
1 tbsp. of ginger powder or pureed

ginger
4 cups of chicken broth
2 tbsp. of coconut oil to taste

DIRECTIONS

- Start by hitting the sauté button on the Pressure cooker to preheat it.
- Add the coconut oil and add half of the butternut squash cubes to it. Brown it lightly for approximately 5 minutes.
- Add the remaining squash and add the rest of the ingredients.
- Close and lock the Pressure cooker. Press MANUAL button and cook for 10 minutes.
- When the time is over, open the Pressure cooker by using the Quick Release.
- Puree the mixture in a blender.
- Serve and enjoy the delicious, healthy soup.

Cream of Asparagus Soup

(Time: 20 Minutes \ Servings: 4)

INGREDIENTS

½ lb. of fresh asparagus, cut into
    pieces
1 sliced yellow onion
3 chopped or minced cloves of garlic
    cloves
3 tbsp. of coconuts oil

½ tsp. of dried thyme
5 cups of bone broth
1 tbsp. lemon juice and zest
1 tsp. of sea salt
2 cups of organic sour cream

DIRECTIONS

- Prepare the asparagus, onion, and garlic. Remove the woody ends from the asparagus stalks and discard it. Chop the asparagus into 1-inch pieces.
- Slice the onion into halves and chop it. Smash the garlic cloves or chop it. Then set the ingredients aside and place the stainless-steel bowl inside the Pressure cooker without putting the lid on. Set to SAUTÉ and add the coconut oil; then add the onions and the garlic.
- Cook the mixture for 5 minutes and stir occasionally; add the thyme and cook for 1 more minute. Add the broth, asparagus, and lemon zest with the salt.

- Then lock the lid of the Pressure cooker and press SOUP mode. Set the pressure timer to 5 minutes, and when the timer goes off, add the sour cream and stir after the Pressure cooker releases the steam.

Beef and Broccoli Stew

(Time: 35 Minutes \ Servings: 4-5)

INGREDIENTS

1 lb. of beef stew meat
1 large quartered onion
½ cup of beef or bone broth
¼ cup of coconut aminos
2 tbsp. of fish sauce

2 large minced cloves of garlic
1 tsp. of ground ginger
½ tsp. of salt
1 tbsp. of coconuts oil
¼ lb. of frozen broccoli

DIRECTIONS

- In the Pressure cooker, place all ingredients except the broccoli. Lock the lid. Press the MEAT button and cook for 35 minutes.
- When the timer goes off, carefully release the pressure and open the lid. Add the broccoli to the inner pot. Place the lid loosely.
- Let the ingredients simmer for around 15 minutes. Serve and enjoy the stew.

Ginger and Sesame Asparagus Stew

(Time: 40 Minutes \ Servings: 3)

INGREDIENTS

8 oz. of diagonally sliced asparagus
2 tbsp. of hoisin sauce
1 ½ tsp. of rice wine
1 tsp. of sesame oil
1 tbsp. of coconut oil
1 tsp. of sesame seeds

1 tsp. of chia powder
2 tsp. of minced and peeled ginger
2 minced garlic cloves
3 coarsely cut carrots
½ tsp. of coarse salt
½ cup of coconut milk.

DIRECTIONS

- In the Pressure cooker, pour the coconut oil with ½ cup of water and add the asparagus. Press SAUTÉ in the setting and set the timer to 5 minutes.
- When the timer goes off, cancel SAUTÉ and add the rest of the ingredients. Lock the lid and set the timer to 35 minutes on BEANS mode.
- Let the ingredients boil, and when the timer goes off, release the pressure. Serve and enjoy the stew.

Broccoli and Fenugreek Stew

(Time: 25 Minutes \ Servings: 4-5)

INGREDIENTS

4 cups of chicken broth
1 cup of coconut milk
4 cups of uncooked egg noodles
4 cups of frozen broccoli florets
½ cup of shredded Asiago cheese
2 diced carrots
¼ tsp. of salt

¼ tsp. of garlic powder
½ cup of cubed butter
1 tbsp. of canola oil
1 tbsp. of coconut oil
1 tsp. of Fenugreek
½ cup of chick peas

DIRECTIONS

- In the Pressure cooker, pour the coconut oil, add the broth, fenugreek, chickpeas, and noodles. Add the broccoli and coconut milk; then press the SOUP mode.
- Add the rest of the ingredients. Lock the lid and set the timer to 15 minutes.
- Once the timer goes off; release the pressure and add ¼ cup of cheese with the garlic powder and let the broth boil for 5 minutes.

Chicken Recipes

Chicken Wings

(Time: 35 minutes \ Servings: 5)

INGREDIENTS:

3 chicken breasts, cut into 2 inch pieces
1 teaspoon garlic powder
1 cup all-purpose flour
2 tablespoons coriander, chopped

½ teaspoon salt
½ teaspoon chili pepper
½ teaspoon cinnamon powder
1 cup oil, for frying
¼ cup water

DIRECTIONS:

- In a bowl, combine flour, salt, chili powder, cumin powder, coriander and toss well.
- Add water and make a thick paste.
- Heat oil in the Pressure cooker on SAUTÉ mode.
- Dip each chicken piece into the flour mixture and then put into the oil.
- Fry each chicken wing until golden and place on a paper towel to drain out the excessive oil.
- Transfer to a serving dish and serve with mint sauce.

Hot Chicken Fingers

(Time: 40 minutes \ Servings: 8)

INGREDIENTS:

3 chicken breasts, cut into 1-inch thick strips
1 teaspoon garlic powder
½ cup flour
½ cup bread crumbs

½ teaspoon salt
2 eggs, whisked
½ teaspoon black pepper
½ teaspoon cinnamon powder
1 cup oil, for frying

DIRECTIONS:

- In a platter, combine flour, bread crumbs, salt, pepper, garlic powder and cinnamon powder, mix well.
- Dip each chicken strip into the eggs and roll them out in the flour mixture.
- Set aside.
- Set the Pressure cooker on SAUTÉ mode and heat oil.
- Fry each chicken finger until golden and place on a paper towel.
- Drain out the excessive oil.
- Transfer to a serving dish and serve with ketchup.

Whole Chicken

(Time: 70 minutes \ Servings: 6)

INGREDIENTS:

1 white chicken
1 teaspoon garlic paste
1 teaspoon ginger paste
1 teaspoon salt
1 teaspoon cayenne pepper
¼ teaspoon chili powder
½ teaspoon black pepper

½ teaspoon cinnamon powder
½ teaspoon cumin powder
3 tablespoons lemon juice
2 tablespoons apple cider vinegar
2 tablespoons soya sauce
3 tablespoons olive oil

DIRECTIONS:

- In a bowl, combine vinegar, cayenne pepper, lemon juice, ginger garlic paste, salt, pepper, chili powder, olive oil, cumin powder and cinnamon powder, mix well.
- Pour over the chicken and rub with all over hands.
- Put the chicken in a greased Pressure cooker and cover up with a lid.
- Cook on SLOW COOK mode for 65-70 minutes.

Chicken Nuggets

(Time: 25 minutes \ Servings: 6)

INGREDIENTS:

2 chicken breasts, cut into small
   pieces
1 teaspoon garlic powder
1 teaspoon onion powder
½ cup bread crumbs
1 teaspoon salt

½ teaspoon black pepper
½ teaspoon cinnamon powder
½ teaspoon cumin powder
1 egg, whisked
1 cup oil, for frying

DIRECTIONS:

- In a bowl mix garlic powder, bread crumbs, onion powder, cinnamon powder, salt, pepper and cumin powder.
- Dip the chicken pieces into the whisked egg and roll out onto the bread crumbs mixture.
- Set the Pressure cooker on SAUTÉ mode and heat oil.
- Deep fry each chicken nugget until golden.
- Transfer to a paper towel.
- Serve with boiled rice or any sauce.

Chicken Pepper Noodles

(Time: 35 minutes \ Servings: 4)

INGREDIENTS:

¼ lb. chicken, boneless, cut into small
   pieces
1 package noodles, boiled
1 red bell pepper, chopped
1 green bell pepper, chopped
1 cup sour cream

1 teaspoon rosemary
2-3 garlic cloves garlic, minced
1 teaspoon salt
½ teaspoon black pepper
3 tablespoons butter

DIRECTIONS:

- Melt butter in the Pressure cooker on SAUTÉ mode and fry garlic for 1 minute.
- Add the chicken and stir fry until lightly golden.
- Season with salt and pepper.
- Stir in the bell peppers and sauté for 3-4 minutes.
- Add noodles and cream, toss well. Cook for 5 minutes, on MANUAL mode and then turn off the heat.
- Transfer to a serving dish and serve hot.

Broccoli Chicken

(Time: 45 minutes \ Servings: 3)

INGREDIENTS:

¼ lb. chicken, boneless, cut into small
   pieces
1 cup broccoli florets
2-3 garlic cloves garlic, minced
1 teaspoon salt

½ teaspoon black pepper
3 tablespoons butter
1 cup chicken broth
2 cup cream

DIRECTIONS:

- Melt butter in the Pressure cooker on SAUTÉ mode and fry garlic for 1 minute.
- Add the chicken and stir fry until golden
- Season with salt and pepper.
- Add broccoli and cream and pour in the chicken broth.
- Cook on MANUAL mode for 10 minutes.

Simple Chicken Wings

(Time: 20 minutes \ Servings: 4)

INGREDIENTS:

2 lb. chicken wings –

1 cup BBQ sauce –

DIRECTIONS:

- Put the chicken wings in the pressure cooker and cover them with the BBQ sauce.
- Cover the lid and cook on MANUAL for 20 minutes.
- When ready, serve and enjoy the delicious wings.

Delicious Chicken

(Time: 15 minutes \ Servings: 3)

INGREDIENTS:

2 cups chicken broth
2 chicken breasts, diced
4 green chilies, chopped
1 onion, chopped
4 potatoes, diced
1 bell pepper, sliced

2 garlic cloves minced
½ tbsp. cumin powder
½ cup tomato sauce
Taco seasoning
Salt to taste

DIRECTIONS:

- Add chicken broth into the pressure cooker and cook for 5 minutes.
- Mix in the green chilies, onion, potatoes, garlic cloves, bell pepper and salt.
- Add cumin powder with chicken breasts and cook for 10 minutes on POULTRY mode.
- Mix in the tomato sauce and stir well.
- When ready, serve with the taco seasoning and enjoy!

Ground Chicken

(Time: 15 minutes \ Servings: 4)

INGREDIENTS:

2 lb. ground chicken
½ cup breadcrumbs
½ cup Cheese, shredded
1 onion, chopped
salt and pepper, to taste
3 garlic cloves, minced

½ bunch parsley, chopped
1 egg
2 cups chicken broth
2 tbsp. vegetable oil
2 tbsp. lemon juice
½ cup sour cream

DIRECTIONS:

- Mix ground chicken with onion, salt, garlic, parsley and lemon juice in a bowl. Mix it well with a spoon or your hand. Whisk the egg in another bowl.
- Add vegetable oil in the pressure cooker and press the SAUTÉ button. Meanwhile, make the balls out of the mixture made in step 1.
- Dip them into the egg and then roll them in the breadcrumbs.
- Place each ball into the pressure cooker.

- When all ready, sprinkle the cheese over them and cook for 10 minutes on POULTRY mode.
- Add chicken broth in the pot and cook for another 5 minutes.
- When ready, serve with sour cream and enjoy!

Chicken Breast with Green Onions

(Time: 25 minutes \ Servings: 4)

INGREDIENTS:

4 chicken breast, diced
½ tbsp. soy sauce
2 cups water
½ tbsp. brown sugar
2 tbsp. rice wine vinegar

1 tbsp. sesame oil
2 tbsp. chili garlic sauce
1 tbsp. cornstarch
2 green onions, chopped
½ tbsp. red pepper flakes

DIRECTIONS:

- Add water, soy sauce and rice wine vinegar into the pressure cooker. Let it cook for 10 minutes on SAUTÉ mode.
- Add the chicken pieces. Mix well.
- Add sesame oil, chili garlic sauce, green onions, red pepper flakes and cornstarch.
- Cook on POULTRY mode for 10 minutes.
- When it beeps, take it out and enjoy the saucy chicken.

Chicken Egg Noodles

(Time: 12 minutes \ Servings: 2)

INGREDIENTS:

2 carrots, sliced
4 stalks celery, sliced
1 onion, sliced
1 cup thyme
1 bay leaf

1 lb. chicken thighs
4 cups egg noodles
2 tbsp. lemon juice
½ cup chicken broth
salt and pepper, to taste

DIRECTIONS:

- Add chicken broth into the pressure cooker.
- Mix in the carrots, celery, onion, thyme, bay leaf, lemon juice and chicken thighs.
- Cook for 10 minutes on POULTRY mode. Add egg noodles and cook for another 10 minutes.

Chicken Shallot

(Time: 20 minutes \ Servings: 3)

INGREDIENTS:

1 lb. chicken breast, pieces
2 lemongrass stalks
2 tbsp. ginger, minced
1 carrot, pieces
2 celery stalks, pieces

1 bay leaf
1 shallot, pieces
1 tbsp. chili powder
2 cups baby spinach
salt and pepper, to taste

DIRECTIONS:

- Add chicken breast into the pressure cooker.
- Mix in the lemongrass, ginger, carrot, celery stalks, bay leaf and shallots.
- Add chili powder, baby spinach, and salt and pepper.
- Cook for 20 minutes on POULTRY mode.

Chicken and Beans

(Time: 20 minutes \ Servings: 3)

INGREDIENTS:

1 lb. chicken breast, pieces
1 tsp. chili powder
2 tomatoes, diced
2 cups chicken broth
1 tbsp. cumin powder
1 cup black beans

1 red bell pepper, chopped
2 tbsp. chipotle sauce
1 tbsp. lime juice
cilantro leaves for garnishing
salt and pepper, to taste

DIRECTIONS:

- Add lime juice into the pressure cooker.
- Mix in the chicken breast, chili powder, tomatoes, chicken broth, cumin powder, red bell pepper and chipotle sauce.
- Add black beans with salt and pepper.
- Cook for 20 minutes on POULTRY mode.

Chicken with Sesame oil

(Time: 20 minutes \ Servings: 3)

INGREDIENTS:

1 tbsp. cornstarch
2 egg whites
1 lb. chicken, sliced
1 tbsp. soy sauce
1 tbsp. sesame oil

1 tbsp. wine vinegar
1 tbsp. ginger, grated
2 tbsp. garlic cloves, minced
salt and pepper, to taste

DIRECTIONS:

- Mix cornstarch and egg whites in a bowl.
- Add the mixture into the pressure cooker.
- Mix in the chicken, soy sauce, sesame oil, wine vinegar, ginger, garlic, and salt and pepper.
- Cook for 20 minutes on POULTRY mode.

Chicken Breasts Recipe with Black Beans

(Time: 18 minutes \ Servings: 3)

INGREDIENTS:

2 tbsp. vegetable oil
2 large sweet onions
3 garlic cloves , minced
1 tbsp. cumin powder
2 tbsp. oregano powder

2 tomatoes , diced
3 chicken breasts , diced
2 cups black beans
2 cups cheddar cheese, grated
Salt to taste

DIRECTIONS:

- Heat the pressure cooker and add vegetable oil.
- Add garlic with the chicken breast pieces. Let it cook for 5 minutes.
- Now add cumin powder, sweet onion, oregano powder, salt and black beans.
- Mix well. Cook on POULTRY mode for 14 minutes.
- When ready, serve by spreading cheddar cheese over it.

Boneless Chicken with Peanut Butter

(Time: 18 minutes \ Servings: 3)

INGREDIENTS:

½ tbsp. canola oil
1 lb. boneless chicken, cut into small
    pieces
1 cup chicken broth
1 tbsp. peanut butter
2 tbsp. soy sauce

½ cup cilantro , chopped
1 tbsp. lime juice
1 tbsp. red pepper flakes
2 tbsp. cornstarch
green onions for garnishing

DIRECTIONS:

- Add canola oil into the pressure cooker and press the SAUTÉ button.
- Mix in the chicken broth with the boneless chicken pieces.
- Cook for 10 minutes POULTRY mode.
- Meanwhile, put the peanut butter, cilantro, lime juice, soy sauce, red pepper flakes and cornstarch in a bowl.
- Stir well.

- Add peanut butter mixture into the pressure cooker and cook for another 4 minutes.
- When done, serve and enjoy with a garnish of green onion!

Chicken Mushroom Mix

(Time: 14 minutes \ Servings: 2)

INGREDIENTS:

3 cups chicken, shredded
1 tbsp. oil
1 onion, chopped
6 small mushrooms, chopped
2 minced garlic cloves

1 cup spinach
½ cup parsley, chopped
2 cups milk
Salt and pepper, to taste
Almonds for seasoning

DIRECTIONS:

- Place chicken into a bowl.
- Mix in the onion, mushrooms, garlic, spinach and parsley.
- Blend well. Add milk and salt and pepper.
- Get a round baking tray.
- Grease it with oil. Add the mixture.
- Cook it in the pressure cooker for 10 minutes on POULTRY mode.
- When ready, serve with almond seasoning!

Chicken Tenders with Garlic

(Time: 13 minutes \ Servings: 2)

INGREDIENTS:

1 lb. chicken tenders
2 garlic cloves, minced
2 tbsp. paprika
2 tbsp. oregano powder
2 tbsp. oil
1 onion, chopped

2 cups peas, frozen
1 cup all-purpose, flour
1 cup chicken stock
1 Egg
Salt and pepper, to taste

DIRECTIONS:

- Add oil into the pressure cooker.
- Mix in the chicken tenders, garlic, paprika, oregano, onion, peas, flour and chicken stock.
- Add egg with salt and pepper. Cook for 10 minutes on POULTRY mode.

Creamy Chicken Noodles

(Time: 30 minutes \ Servings: 5)

INGREDIENTS:

¼ lb. chicken, boneless, pieces, boiled
1 package noodles, boiled
1 teaspoon tarragon
1 cup cream
¼ cup all-purpose flour
½ cup milk

1 teaspoon rosemary
2-3 garlic cloves garlic, minced
1 teaspoon salt
½ teaspoon black pepper
3 tablespoons butter

DIRECTIONS:

- Melt butter in the Pressure cooker on SAUTÉ mode and fry garlic for 1 minute.
- Add in cream and flour, stir continuously.
- Pour milk by continuously stirring.
- Transfer the chicken and combine well. Season with salt and pepper.
- Now spread noodles into a platter and top with the creamy chicken.
- Sprinkle tarragon and serve.

Hot Chicken Chili

(Time: 25 minutes \ Servings: 3)

INGREDIENTS:

2 chicken breasts
1 cup chili garlic sauce
¼ cup tomato ketchup
4 tablespoons honey
2 tablespoons soya sauce

2 tomatoes, chopped
¼ teaspoon salt
¼ teaspoon cayenne pepper
3 tablespoons olive oil

DIRECTIONS:

- Combine the chili garlic sauce, tomato ketchup, soya sauce, honey, salt, and pepper and mix.Pour the sauce over the chicken and toss well.
- Heat oil in the Pressure cooker on SAUTÉ mode and add in the chicken breasts.
- Cover and cook on POULTRY mode for 20 minutes.
- Transfer to a serving dish and serve.

Hot Garlic Chicken Breasts

(Time: 35 minutes \ Servings: 5)

INGREDIENTS:

2 chicken breasts
2 tablespoons apple cider vinegar

1 cup tomato ketchup
1 teaspoon garlic powder

¼ teaspoon salt
½ teaspoon chili powder

3 tablespoons olive oil

DIRECTIONS:

- Combine the vinegar, ketchup, chili powder, salt, and garlic powder.
- Drizzle over the chicken and toss well.
- Set the Pressure cooker on SAUTÉ mode and heat oil.
- Transfer the chicken breasts in the pot. Cook for 35 minutes.

Chicken and Lentil Meal

(Time: 70 minutes \ Servings: 5)

INGREDIENTS:

2 chicken breasts, boiled, shredded
1 cup yellow lentil, soaked
1 cup split gram, soaked overnight
¼ teaspoon garlic paste
½ teaspoon salt
1 onion, sliced

1 tomato, chopped
¼ teaspoon turmeric powder
½ teaspoon chili powder
2 tablespoons oil
¼ cup olive oil, for frying
3 cups water

DIRECTIONS:

- Heat the oil in the Pressure cooker on SAUTÉ mode and fry onion until golden.
- Spread the onion on paper towel and set aside.
- In the same pot, add lentils, water, and turmeric powder and boil on BEANS mode for 30 minutes.
- Transfer the shredded chicken and boiled lentils into a blender and blend to a puree.
- In the Pressure cooker, add 2 tablespoons of cooking oil and fry garlic for 30 seconds until lightly golden.
- Add tomatoes, chili powder, and salt and stir fry for 5-6 minutes.
- Add in the chicken lentils' puree and let simmer for 10 minutes.

Chicken Mince and Peas

(Time: 35 minutes \ Servings: 5)

INGREDIENTS:

1 cup chicken mince
1 cup peas
1 onion, chopped
2-3 garlic cloves, minced
¼ teaspoon cumin powder
¼ teaspoon cinnamon powder
2 tomatoes, chopped

1 teaspoon salt
½ teaspoon chili powder
2 tablespoons olive oil
1 bunch coriander, chopped
½ cup chicken broth

94

DIRECTIONS:

- Heat oil in the Pressure cooker on SAUTÉ mode; fry garlic and onion for 1 minute. Add the ground chicken and stir fry until its color is slightly changed. Season with salt and chili powder. Stir in tomatoes and sauté for 3-4 minutes.
- Now add the peas and fry until soft. Add the chicken broth on and cook on MANUAL mode for 15 minutes. Sprinkle cumin powder and cinnamon powder. Place on a serving dish and top with coriander.

Chicken with Avocado Cream

(Time: 35 minutes \ Servings: 6)

INGREDIENTS

4 lb. of organic chicken
1 tbsp. of coconut Oil
1 tsp. of paprika
1 ½ cups of Pacific Chicken Bone Broth
1 tsp. of dried thyme

¼ tsp. of freshly ground black pepper
1 tsp. of ginger
2 tbsp. of lemon juice
½ tsp. of sea salt
6 cloves of peeled garlic
1 Avocado

DIRECTIONS

- In a medium bowl, combine the paprika, thyme, salt, dried ginger, and pepper. Then rub the seasoning over the outer parts of the chicken.
- Heat the oil in the Cooker and let it simmer. Add the chicken breast side down and cook it for 6 minutes.
- Now, flip the chicken and add the broth, lemon juice, and garlic cloves. Lock the lid and set the timer to 30 minutes on POULTRY mode.
- Prepare the avocado cream by whisking the contents of the avocado with 2 tbsp. of coconut oil and ½ tsp. of salt. Once the timer beeps, naturally release the pressure.
- Remove the chicken from the Cooker and set it aside for 5 minutes before serving it.

Chicken with Sweet Potatoes

(Time: 30 minutes \ Servings: 4)

INGREDIENTS

2 cups of cubed and peeled sweet potatoes
2 tbsp. of coconut oil
1 lb. of skinless and boneless cubed chicken breast halves
3 minced cloves of garlic
6 tbsp. of tamari soy sauce
1 cup of water

3 tbsp. of honey
3 tbsp. of hot sauce
1 peeled and diced mango
¼ tsp. of smashed red pepper flakes
1 tsp. of cornstarch
1 tsp. of ginger
1 cup of warm water

DIRECTIONS

- Start by placing the sweet potatoes in the Cooker and pour enough water so the potatoes are covered. Cook for 10 minutes on POULTRY mode.
- Seal the lid, and when the timer goes off, quickly release the pressure and drain the potatoes.
- Place 2 tbsp. of coconut oil in the Pressure cooker and add the chicken. Sauté for 5 minutes. Sprinkle the ginger and garlic and cook for several more minutes. Add the tamari, a cup of warm water, and the honey with the hot sauce.
- Add the cornstarch to the mixture and set on Boil feature for 10 minutes. Serve and enjoy a healthy chicken lunch with sweet potatoes.

Asian Style Chicken

(Time: 9 minutes \ Servings: 4)

INGREDIENTS

½ cup of slivered almonds
1 tbsp. of coconut oil
1 tbsp. of toasted sesame oil
4 minced cloves of garlic
1 tbsp. of minced fresh ginger
1 lb. of boneless and skinless chicken breasts

½ onion
2 carrots
2 celery ribs, diced
¼ cup of hoisin sauce mixed with 2 tbsp. of water
1 tbsp. of soy sauce
cooked rice or quinoa

DIRECTIONS

- Toast the slivered almonds and set aside. Heat the oils in the Pressure cooker and add the garlic and ginger. Press SAUTÉ and set the timer to 5 minutes.
- Add the chicken and brown it on both sides; then add the rest of the ingredients except the rice.
- Close the lid and set it to POULTRY mode for around 7 minutes.
- Once the timer goes off, release the pressure of the Pressure cooker.
- Serve the chicken with the cooked rice or quinoa.
- Pour the sauce and garnish with almonds.

Chicken with Ginger and Broccolini

(Time: 15 minutes \ Servings: 3)

INGREDIENTS

6 tbsp. of sake
6 tbsp. of low soy sauce
¼ cup of granulated sugar
2 tbsp. of coconut oil
1 lb. of boneless, skinless chicken

thighs
1 pinch of kosher salt
1 pinch freshly ground black pepper
1 lb. of broccoli florets cut it into long pieces

3 thinly sliced white and green
   scallions

4 minced garlic cloves or very thinly

sliced

1 piece of sliced, peeled ginger

DIRECTIONS

- Mix the soy sauce with the sugar into a medium-size bowl and keep stirring until the sugar is perfectly combined; then set aside.
- Press SAUTÉ and heat the coconut oil on for 2-3 minutes.
- Add the chicken things and make sure to flip half way to get a golden color.
- Once you finish sautéing the chicken, add the mixture, broccoli, and scallion whites.
- Arrange the chicken on top of the broccoli.
- Pour 1 cup of water into the Pressure cooker and add the garlic and ginger.
- Close the lid and set the feature function to MANUAL for 10 minutes.
- Season with salt and pepper and serve it with scallion greens.

Red Meat

Pork Steaks

(Time: 65 minutes \ Servings: 5)

INGREDIENTS:

2 pork fillets
1 teaspoon garlic powder
½ teaspoon chili powder
2 tablespoons soya sauce
4 tablespoons barbecue sauce

¼ teaspoon turmeric powder
1 teaspoon salt
2 tablespoons vinegar
4 tablespoons olive oil

DIRECTIONS:

- In a bowl, add vinegar, soya sauce, barbecue sauce, chili powder, salt, garlic powder and oil.
- Transfer to the Pressure cooker and cook on MEAT mode for 45 minutes.

Mutton Gravy

(Time: 45 minutes \ Servings: 4)

INGREDIENTS:

½ lb mutton, boiled
1 cup tomato puree
1-inch ginger slice
½ teaspoon garlic paste
1 teaspoon salt

¼ teaspoon chili powder
1 cup water
½ teaspoon cumin powder
4 tablespoons oil

DIRECTIONS:

- Heat oil in the Pressure cooker on SAUTÉ mode and fry tomatoes with chili powder, ginger, garlic and salt, for 5-10 minute. Add mutton and fry well.
- Add in water and cook on MEAT mode for 20 minutes.
- Sprinkle cumin powder and transfer to a serving dish.

Ground Meat Lemonade

(Time: 40 minutes \ Servings: 3)

INGREDIENTS:

2 cups beef mince
1 teaspoon salt
2 tablespoons lemon juice
¼ teaspoon chili powder

2 tomatoes, chopped
2-3 garlic cloves, minced
4 tablespoons oil

DIRECTIONS:

- Heat oil in the Pressure cooker and stir-fry garlic for 30 seconds. Add the mince and fry well until its color changes.
- Season with salt and pepper.
- Add tomatoes and stir fry for 10-15 minutes with a few splashes of water.
- Drizzle lemon juice on top.

Beef with Peas

(Time: 17 minutes \ Servings: 2)

INGREDIENTS:

2 tbsp. olive oil
1 lb. ground beef
1 tbsp. lemon juice
2 tbsp. butter

2 cups peas, frozen
1 onion, chopped
2 garlic cloves, minced
salt and pepper, to taste

DIRECTIONS:

- Heat oil and add garlic into the pressure cooker. Stir-fry for 1-2 minutes.
- Mix in the lemon juice, butter, onion, beef, peas, salt and pepper. Keep stirring for 1-2 minutes. Close the lid and cook for 15 minutes on MEAT mode.
- When ready, serve and enjoy!

Diced Meat with Potatoes

(Time: 22 minutes \ Servings: 3)

INGREDIENTS:

2 tbsp. oil
2 tbsp. soy sauce
1 lb. meat , diced
2 garlic cloves, minced
2 jalapeno peppers, chopped

2 cups potatoes diced
1 cup broth, any
salt and pepper, to taste
cilantro and peanuts for garnishing

DIRECTIONS:

- Heat oil into the pressure cooker.
- Mix in the soy sauce, meat, garlic, jalapeno peppers and potatoes.
- Add broth with salt and pepper.
- Cook for 20 minutes on MEAT mode.
- When ready, serve with cilantro and peanuts dressing.

Simple Meatballs Recipe

(Time: 17 minutes \ Servings: 3)

INGREDIENTS:

1 lb. beef
½ onion, diced
1 carrot, diced
2 sticks celery, diced
3 garlic cloves, minced

1 cup marsala wine
2 cups beef broth
2 tomatoes, diced
½ tbsp. tomato paste
salt and pepper, to taste

DIRECTIONS:

- Press SAUTÉ and add carrot, onion, and celery.
- Remove from pot and keep it aside in a bowl.
- Now add garlic, Marsala wine, tomatoes, beef, and salt and pepper into the bowl.
- Mix well and make small balls out of it.
- Add beef broth and tomato paste into the pressure cooker.
- Place the meat balls in the pot.
- Let it cook for 10 minutes on MEAT mode.
- When ready, serve!

Sweet Potatoes with Meat

(Time: 24 minutes \ Servings: 4)

INGREDIENTS:

2 tbsp. olive oil
2 sweet potatoes, diced
2 onion, diced
2 carrots, diced
1 lb. red meat, in chunks
3 garlic cloves, minced

1 tbsp. chili powder
1 tbsp. chipotle powder
1 tsp. cumin powder
2 tomatoes , diced
2 tbsp. lime juice
salt to taste

DIRECTIONS:

- Add oil into the pressure cooker and select the option for SAUTÉ.
- When it heats up lightly, add onion, garlic cloves, lime juice and red meat. Let it cook for 10 minutes.
- Now add chili powder, carrots, cumin powder, chipotle powder and salt.
- Add sweet potatoes and cook for 10 minutes on MEAT mode When it beeps, take it out and serve.

Diced Meat with Onions

(Time: 15 minutes \ Servings: 2)

INGREDIENTS:

1 large onion, sliced
1 tbsp. olive oil
1 lb. red meat , diced

2 tomatoes, chopped
½ tbsp. chili powder
salt and pepper, to taste

DIRECTIONS:

- Add onion and olive oil into the pressure cooker and press the SAUTÉ button.
- Mix in the tomatoes, red meat, chili powder, and salt and pepper.
- Cook for 10 minutes MEAT mode.
- When ready, serve with bread or a favorite side dish!

Meat with Peppers

(Time: 15 minutes \ Servings: 2)

INGREDIENTS:

1 tbsp. vegetable oil
½ cup tomato sauce
1 lb. ground meat
2 green peppers, sliced
2 red peppers, sliced

1 onion , chopped
2 garlic cloves, chopped
½ tbsp. chili powder
salt and pepper, to taste

DIRECTIONS:

- Add garlic, onion and vegetable oil into the pressure cooker. Press the SAUTÉ button. Mix in the ground meat, green peppers and red peppers.
- Sprinkle salt, pepper and chili powder on the meat. Cook for 15 minutes MEAT mode.

Hot Shredded Pork

(Time: 30 minutes \ Servings: 4)

INGREDIENTS:

2 pork fillets, boiled, shredded
½ teaspoon garlic paste
½ teaspoon salt
½ teaspoon soya sauce
2 tablespoons lemon juice

2 tablespoons barbecue sauce
½ cup chili garlic sauce
2 tablespoons vinegar
½ teaspoon chili powder
2 tablespoons oil

DIRECTIONS:

- Heat oil on SAUTÉ mode and fry garlic for 1 minute.
- Place the pork and brown well.

- Add soya sauce, chili garlic sauce, vinegar, barbecue sauce, salt, and chili powder and fry well.
- Transfer to a serving dish and drizzle lemon juice.

Pork Chops Gravy

(Time: 55 minutes \ Servings: 5)

INGREDIENTS:

½ lb. pork chops
1 onion, chopped
2-3 garlic cloves, minced
2 tomatoes, chopped
¼ teaspoon turmeric powder
¼ teaspoon cumin powder

¼ teaspoon cinnamon powder
1 teaspoon salt
½ teaspoon chili powder
4 tablespoons olive oil
½ cup chicken broth
1 green chili

DIRECTIONS:

- Heat oil on SAUTÉ mode and fry onion for 1 minute.
- Add in the tomatoes, chili powder, salt, and turmeric powder and fry.
- Now add the pork chops and brown them for 5-10 minutes on high heat.
- Add the chicken broth on and cook on MANUAL mode for 10-15 minutes.
- Sprinkle cumin powder and cinnamon powder, toss well.
- Place to a serving dish and enjoy.

Beef Okra

(Time: 35 minutes \ Servings: 4)

INGREDIENTS:

½ lb. mutton, boiled
1 cup okra
1 onion, chopped
2-3 garlic cloves, minced
2 tomatoes, chopped

¼ teaspoon turmeric powder
1 teaspoon salt
½ teaspoon chili powder
4 tablespoons olive oil

DIRECTIONS:

- Heat oil in the Pressure cooker and fry the okra until crispy; then set aside.
- In the same pot, fry onion for 1 minute.
- Add in the tomatoes, chili powder, salt, turmeric powder and fry.
- Now add the mutton and stir fry for 10 minutes on MEAT mode.
- Then add the okra and mix well. Transfer to a serving dish.

Slow Cooked Zucchini and Pork

(Time: 60 minutes \ Servings: 5)

INGREDIENTS:

½ lb. pork, pieces
2 zucchini, sliced
3 turnips, peeled, diced
1 onion, chopped
2-3 garlic cloves, minced

2 tomatoes, chopped
¼ teaspoon turmeric powder
1 teaspoon salt
½ teaspoon chili powder
4 tablespoons olive oil

DIRECTIONS:

- In the Pressure cooker, add all ingredients and toss.
- Cook for 60 minutes on SLOW COOK mode.

Beefalo Wings

(Time: 45 minutes \ Servings: 4)

INGREDIENTS:

2 lean meat fillets, cut into strips
1 teaspoon garlic powder
½ cup all-purpose flour
½ teaspoon salt

½ teaspoon chili powder
½ teaspoon cinnamon powder
1 cup oil, for frying
1 egg, whisked

DIRECTIONS:

- In a bowl, combine flour, salt, chili powder, garlic, cumin powder, and pepper, and toss around.
- Dip each meat strip into the whisked egg and roll out into the flour mixture.
- Heat oil in the Pressure cooker on SAUTÉ mode.
- Transfer the meat into the oil and fry until golden.
- Place on a paper towel to remove the excess oil.
- Serve with any sauce.

Pressure cooker Beef Rice

(Time: 45 minutes \ Servings: 5)

INGREDIENTS:

2 cups rice, soaked
½ lb. beef, boiled, pieces
1 teaspoon cumin seeds
1 bay leaf
2 garlic cloves, minced
1 teaspoon black pepper
1 pinch turmeric powder

1 teaspoon cumin powder
2 tomatoes, chopped
2 medium onions, sliced
1 teaspoon salt
3 tablespoons olive oil
4 cups chicken broth

DIRECTIONS:

- Heat oil in the Pressure cooker on SAUTÉ mode, fry onion until golden. Add the tomatoes, cumin seeds and bay leaf and fry well.
- Then add the beef and season with salt, turmeric powder, pepper, and garlic and fry well.
- Pour in the vegetable broth and add cumin powder, and cinnamon powder, boil.
- Add rice and let it simmer until bubbles appear on the surface, then cover the pot with a lid. Cook on medium heat for 20 minutes on RICE mode. Transfer to a serving dish and enjoy.

Hot and Spicy Beef Gravy

(Time: 40 minutes \ Servings: 4)

INGREDIENTS:

½ lb. meat, cut into small pieces, boneless
1 cup tomato puree
1 onion, chopped
¼ garlic paste
1 teaspoon salt

½ teaspoon chili powder
½ teaspoon cumin powder
½ teaspoon cinnamon powder
¼ teaspoon turmeric powder
2 tablespoons olive oil

DIRECTIONS:

- Heat oil in the Pressure cooker on SAUTÉ mode and fry garlic and onion for a minute.
- Add the tomato puree, salt, chili powder, and turmeric powder and fry again for 4-5 minutes.
- Add in the boiled meat and stir fry well on MEAT mode for 10-15 minutes.
- Sprinkle cumin powder and cinnamon powder and mix well.

Red Beans Tendered Beef

(Time: 120 minutes \ Servings: 4)

INGREDIENTS:

1 can red beans
½ lb. beef meat, pieces
2 tomatoes, slices
1 cup spring onion, chopped
1 teaspoon salt

1 teaspoon chili powder
1 teaspoon garlic powder
2 tablespoons olive oil
3 cups vegetables broth

DIRECTIONS:

- In the Pressure cooker, add all ingredients and toss well.
- Cook on low heat for 2 hours on SLOW COOK mode.

Meat Pops

(Time: 25 minutes \ Servings: 6)

INGREDIENTS:

1 meat fillet, cut into small pieces
1 teaspoon garlic powder
1 teaspoon onion powder
½ cup flour
¼ cup water

1 teaspoon salt
½ teaspoon black pepper
½ teaspoon cinnamon powder
½ teaspoon cumin powder
1 cup oil, for frying

DIRECTIONS:

- In a bowl, mix flour, water, garlic powder, bread crumbs, onion powder, cinnamon powder, salt, pepper, and cumin powder. Set the Pressure cooker on SAUTÉ mode and heat oil. Dip the meat pieces into the flour mixture.
- Deep fry each meat pop until golden.

Pulled Beef

(Time: 30 minutes \ Servings: 4)

INGREDIENTS:

2 beef fillets, boiled, shredded
½ teaspoon garlic paste
½ teaspoon salt
½ teaspoon soya sauce
2 tablespoons barbecue sauce

½ cup chili garlic sauce
2 tablespoons vinegar
½ teaspoon chili powder
2 tablespoons oil

DIRECTIONS:

- Heat oil in the Pressure cooker on SAUTÉ mode and fry garlic for 1 minute.
- Transfer the beef and fry well. Add soya sauce, chili garlic sauce, vinegar, barbecue sauce, salt, and chili powder and fry well.

Roasted Bell Pepper with Beef

(Time: 120 minutes \ Servings: 4)

INGREDIENTS:

4 yellow and red bell peppers, halved, seeds
½ lb. beef, boiled
½ teaspoon garlic powder

½ teaspoon salt
½ teaspoon black pepper
3 tablespoons olive oil

DIRECTIONS:

- In the Pressure cooker, add all ingredients and toss well.
- Cook on low heat for 2 hours on SLOW COOK mode.

Beef and Peas Gravy

(Time: 45 minutes \ Servings: 5)

INGREDIENTS:

½ lb. beef, boiled
1 cup peas
1 onion, chopped
2-3 garlic cloves, minced
2 tomatoes, chopped
¼ teaspoon turmeric powder
¼ teaspoon cumin powder

¼ teaspoon cinnamon powder
1 teaspoon salt
½ teaspoon chili powder
2 tablespoons olive oil
½ cup chicken broth
1 green chili

DIRECTIONS:

- Heat oil in the Pressure cooker on sauté mode and fry onion for 1 minute.
- Add in the tomatoes, chili powder, salt, and turmeric powder and fry.
- Add the beef and stir fry well.
- Then add the peas and fry for 5-6 minutes.
- Add the chicken broth and green chili and cook on CHILI mode for 15 minutes.
- Sprinkle cumin powder and cinnamon powder, toss well.

Beef and Chickpea Stew

(Time: 35 minutes \ Servings: 4)

INGREDIENTS:

½ lb. beef, boneless, pieces
1 cup chickpea, boiled
1 tomato, chopped
1 onion, chopped
1 teaspoon garlic paste
¼ teaspoon ginger paste
¼ teaspoon turmeric powder
¼ teaspoon salt

¼ teaspoon chili powder
¼ teaspoon cayenne pepper
1 carrot, sliced
¼ teaspoon cinnamon powder
½ teaspoon cumin powder
3 cups chicken broth
2 tablespoons olive oil

DIRECTIONS:

- Heat oil on SAUTÉ mode and add fry onion until transparent.
- Add in garlic, ginger, tomatoes, salt, cayenne pepper, chili powder, turmeric powder and fry for 4-5 minutes. Add the beef and stir fry on MEAT mode for 15 minutes with a few splashes of water.
- Now add the chickpea and carrots and stir-fry for 5 minutes.
- Transfer the chicken broth, cover with a lid, and cook on MANUAL mode for 30 minutes.
- Sprinkle cumin powder and cinnamon powder. Transfer to serving dish and enjoy.

Carrot and Beef Stew

(Time: 45 minutes \ Servings: 4)

INGREDIENTS:

½ lb. beef, pieces
3 carrots, peeled, sliced
1 tomato, chopped
1 onion, chopped
1 teaspoon garlic paste
¼ teaspoon ginger paste
¼ teaspoon turmeric powder

¼ teaspoon salt
¼ teaspoon chili powder
¼ teaspoon cinnamon powder
½ teaspoon cumin powder
3 cups chicken broth
2 tablespoons olive oil

DIRECTIONS:

- Heat oil on SAUTÉ mode and add fry onion until transparent.
- Stir in garlic, ginger, tomatoes, salt, chili powder, and turmeric powder and fry for 6 minutes.
- Stir fry the beef for 5-6 minutes. Now add the chickpea and stir fry for 5 minutes.
- Transfer the chicken broth, cover with a lid and cook on MANUAL mode for 40 minutes. Sprinkle cumin powder and cinnamon powder. Transfer to a serving dish and serve.

Fried Okra with Beef

(Time: 45 minutes \ Servings: 4)

INGREDIENTS:

¼ lb. beef, boiled, boneless
1 cup okra, sliced
1 tomato, chopped
1 onion, sliced
1 teaspoon garlic paste
¼ teaspoon ginger paste

¼ teaspoon turmeric powder
¼ teaspoon salt
¼ teaspoon chili powder
3 cups chicken broth
¼ cup olive oil

DIRECTIONS:

- Heat oil on SAUTÉ mode and fry okra until golden.
- Transfer to a platter and set aside.
- In the same pot, add onion and fry until transparent.
- Stir in garlic, ginger, tomatoes, salt, chili powder, and turmeric powder and fry for 6 minutes.
- Stir-fry the beef for 5-6 minutes.
- Now add the fried okra and stir-fry for 10-15 minutes.
- Sprinkle cumin powder and cinnamon powder.
- Transfer to a serving dish,.

Beef Meat with Shallots

(Time: 20 minutes \ Servings: 3)

INGREDIENTS

¾ lb. of halved, peeled shallots
1 ½ tbsp. of olive oil
3 cups of beef broth
¾ cup of red wine
1 ½ tsp. tomato paste

2 lb. of trimmed beef tenderloin roast
1 tsp. of dried thyme
3 tbsp. of coconut oil
1 tbsp. of almond flour
salt and pepper, to taste

DIRECTIONS

- Heat the Mueller pressure cooker on medium heat and melt 1 tbsp. of olive oil. SAUTÉ and season with salt and pepper.
- Roast the shallots and mix the wine and beef broth. Press MANUAL and cook for 20 minutes.
- Close the lid, and when the timer beeps, quick release the pressure with a towel. Add the tomato paste. Pat the beef dry and sprinkle salt and pepper on it.
- Add the thyme, salt, pepper, and drizzle with coconut oil.
- Then pour ½ cup of water and brown the beef on each side for 15 minutes.
- Once cooked, add the broth mixture, 1 ½ tbsp. of coconut oil, and the flour and cook on MEAT mode for 10 more minutes.

Sprouts with Pork Portions

(Time: 20 minutes \ Servings: 2)

INGREDIENTS

¼ lb. of cubed pork
2 tbsp. of coconut oil
1 lb. of halved brussels sprouts
½ chopped onion
1 pinch of salt or to taste
1 pinch of black pepper

1 tsp. of flax seed powder
¼ cup of toasted and chopped almonds
1 lemon zest
½ cup of coconut milk

DIRECTIONS

- Set the Mueller pressure cooker on medium heat and pour the coconut oil in it. Press SAUTÉ and add the pork. Cook for 2-3 minutes. Add the onions, flax seed powder, and Brussels sprouts.
- Add ½ cup of coconut milk and set the Mueller pressure cooker to MEAT mode for 25 minutes.
- Season with pepper and salt. Serve the pork with the chopped mango and avocado with a handful of almonds and a squeeze of a lemon zest.

Lamb with Pomegranate Seeds

(Time: 25 minutes \ Servings: 4)

INGREDIENTS

2 lb. of lamb chops
6 tbsp. of bacon fat
1 chopped onion

1 cup of pomegranate juice
½ tsp. of sea salt
seed of 2 pomegranates

DIRECTIONS

- Heat the Mueller pressure cooker on medium heat and pour 2 cups of water.
- Press MEAT mode and cook for 15 minutes.
- Close the lid and seal the valve.
- Once the timer beeps, release the pressure with the use of a towel.
- Pour 2 tbsp. of coconut oil on the lamb with a pinch of salt and a pinch of pepper.
- Add the onions and press SAUTÉ and cook the lamb for 5 more minutes.
- Keep stirring to avoid burning the lamb. Once the lamb is perfectly cooked, add the pomegranate seeds and cook for 5 minutes.
- Finally, press KEEP WARM button.

Ground Beef with Flax Seeds

(Time: 30 minutes \ Servings: 2)

INGREDIENTS

2 lb. of ground beef
1 package of sausage
2 tsp. of dried, chopped onion
1 tsp. of garlic powder
1 tsp. of dried basil
1 tsp. of dried parsley

½ cup of flax seed meal
½ tsp. of salt
1 tsp. of ground fennel
1 cup of dried slices of tomatoes
2 beaten eggs
1 mango, cubed

DIRECTIONS

- In a deep bowl, mix the onion, garlic powder, dried basil, flax seed meal, salt, and ground fennel.
- Squeeze the sausage out of any casings and place in the bowl cut in very small pieces.
- Place the ground meat in the same bowl and mix the ingredients with hands. Shape the meat into the form of two loaves.
- Heat the Mueller pressure cooker on medium heat and melt a tbsp. of coconut oil.
- Transfer the meat loafs and press Meat mode.
- Close the lid and set the timer for 30 minutes.
- Serve the meat loaves with mango cubes.

Veal Meat with Asparagus and Almonds

(Time: 20 minutes \ Servings: 3)

INGREDIENTS

1 lb. of veal meat
2 tbsp. of lemon juice
¼ tsp. of sea salt
1 pinch of ground black pepper
1 lb. of fresh and trimmed asparagus
2 tbsp. of coconut oil

6 cups of mushrooms
½ cup of green sliced onions
2 tbsp. of toasted and finely chopped
  almonds
3 cloves of minced garlic

DIRECTIONS

- Heat the Mueller pressure cooker and add ½ cup of water or coconut milk. Pour into the juice of 1 lemon, 1 tbsp. of oil, garlic, salt, and pepper. Add the mushrooms and veal meat. Close the lid of the Mueller pressure cooker and press the button MEAT mode and cook for 15 minutes.
- Once the timer beeps, add a tbsp. of oil and asparagus and set on high pressure for 3 minutes. Release the pressure. Add the green onions and sauté for 2 more minutes.
- Remove the ingredients from the Mueller pressure cooker and pour over the lemon juice mixture. Serve the dish and enjoy with a sprinkle of almonds.

Seafood and Fish

Lemon Fish Steaks

(Time: 25 minutes \ Servings: 3)

INGREDIENTS:

4 fish fillets
2 tablespoons extra virgin olive oil
1 teaspoon fine sea salt

1 teaspoon black pepper
Lemon wedges, for serving
2 tablespoons lemon juice

DIRECTIONS:

- Sprinkle salt and pepper on the fish. Drizzle lemon juice and oil, then rub all over.
- Place into a greased Mueller pressure cooker and cook for 15 minutes on STEAM mode.
- Serve with lemon wedges.

Creamy Tilapia

(Time: 25 minutes \ Servings: 3)

INGREDIENTS:

½ lb. oz. tilapia fillets
2 tablespoons lemon juice
½ teaspoon of black pepper
2 tablespoons chopped fresh dill

weed
½ teaspoon salt
Cooking spray

DIRECTIONS:

- Grease the Mueller pressure cooker with a cooking spray and place the fish filets, sprinkle salt and dill.
- Drizzle lemon juice and toss around. Cook for 20 minutes on STEAM mode.
- After that, add cream cheese and black pepper and combine. Simmer for 2 minutes.

Roasted Fish with Vegetables

(Time: 25 minutes \ Servings: 4)

INGREDIENTS:

2 tomatoes, sliced
1 avocado, chopped
1 onion, sliced
1 bunch green coriander, chopped
½ cup tomato puree

1 teaspoon garlic paste
Salt and black pepper, to taste
2 fish fillets, cut into pieces
1 teaspoon lemon juice

111

DIRECTIONS:

- Heat oil in the Mueller pressure cooker and fry garlic and onion for 1 minutes.
- Add the fish and fry until golden. Add tomatoes and keep frying.
- Season with salt and chili powder.
- Now add avocado, tomato puree, and lemon juice, simmer for 10 minutes.
- Sprinkle coriander.
- Transfer to a serving platter and serve.

Creamy Tuna with Macaroni

(Time: 25 minutes \ Servings: 3)

INGREDIENTS:

¼ lb. tuna, cut into pieces
1 cup cream
1 teaspoon garlic paste

Salt and black pepper to taste
1 cup macaroni, boiled

DIRECTIONS:

- Heat oil in the Pressure cooker and fry garlic for about 30 seconds on SAUTÉ mode.
- Add the fish and sauté it for 1-2 minutes. Season with salt and pepper. Stir in the macaroni and cream, mix well. Transfer to a serving platter and serve.

Fried Tuna with Tamarind Sauce

(Time: 25 minutes \ Servings: 3)

INGREDIENTS:

3 tuna fish fillets
2 tablespoons extra-virgin olive oil
1 teaspoon fine sea salt

1 teaspoon black pepper
Lemon wedges, for serving
2 tablespoons lemon juice

DIRECTIONS:

- Sprinkle salt and pepper on the fish. Then drizzle lemon juice and oil, rub all over the fish.
- Place it into a greased Pressure cooker and cook for 15 minutes on STEAM mode.

Crispy Crumb Fish

(Time: 25 minutes \ Servings: 3)

INGREDIENTS:

2 fish fillets
1 cup bread crumbs
1 egg, whisked
½ tablespoon salt

½ tablespoon black pepper
1 teaspoon garlic powder
Oil for frying

DIRECTIONS:

- In a bowl, add the bread crumbs, salt, pepper, and garlic and toss well.
- Dip the fish fillet in the egg and then roll out in the bread crumbs.
- Heat oil in the Pressure cooker and fry fish pieces until golden brown on sauté mode.

Fish Patties

(Time: 35 minutes \ Servings: 3)

INGREDIENTS:

2 fish fillets, cut into pieces
½ tablespoon salt
½ tablespoon black pepper
1 tablespoon coriander, chopped

¼ teaspoon garlic paste
4 tablespoons of gram flour
1 potato, boiled
½ cup oil for frying

DIRECTIONS:

- Heat 2 tablespoons of oil on SAUTÉ mode.
- Fry the fish until lightly golden.
- Now crumble with a fork and place aside.
- Combine the fish, potatoes, garlic, coriander, salt and pepper and mix well.
- Make small round patties with this mixture and place into a platter.
- Heat oil in the Pressure cooker and shallow fry the patties on SAUTÉ mode until lightly golden.

Salmon Bowl

(Time: 15 minutes \ Servings: 2)

INGREDIENTS:

2 salmon fillets, cut into pieces
½ tablespoon salt
½ tablespoon black pepper
¼ teaspoon garlic powder

1 cup lettuce leaves
1 tomato, chopped
2 tablespoons oil

DIRECTIONS:

- Heat oil on sauté mode. Stir fry the lettuce for 1 minute, then set aside.
- In the same pot, fry the fish until lightly golden.
- Season with salt, pepper and garlic powder.
- Transfer to a serving platter and serve with lettuce and tomatoes.

Tarragon Steamed Fish

(Time: 25 minutes \ Servings: 3)

INGREDIENTS:

2 fish fillets, cut into pieces
½ tablespoon salt
½ tablespoon black pepper

2 tablespoons tarragon
¼ teaspoon garlic paste
2 tablespoons oil

DIRECTIONS:

- In the Pressure cooker, place a rack and fill the pot with 2 cups of water.
- Season the fish with salt, pepper, tarragon, and garlic, rub well.
- Place the fish on the rack and cover with a lid.
- Cook for 25 minutes on STEAM mode.

Fish Smash

(Time: 35 minutes \ Servings: 3)

INGREDIENTS:

½ tablespoon salt
3-4 tuna fillets
½ tablespoon black pepper
1 clove of garlic, minced

2 tablespoons oil
1 teaspoon basil, chopped
1 cup cream

DIRECTIONS:

- Heat oil on SAUTÉ mode. Add the fish and fry on low heat. Put on a platter and scramble with a fork.
- Transfer back to the pot and add cream, salt, pepper, and garlic and let it simmer for 2-3 minutes.

Coconut Fish

(Time: 45 minutes \ Servings: 3)

INGREDIENTS:

3-4 fish fillets, pieces
½ tablespoon salt
½ tablespoon chili powder
½ cup coconut, crushed

1 cup coconut milk
1 clove of garlic, minced
Oil for frying
3 oz. boiled rice for serving

DIRECTIONS:

- Take a large bowl and put the fish fillets inside. Sprinkle salt and black pepper and place into a platter.
- Heat oil in Pressure cooker and fry the fish until golden. Heat two tablespoons of oil on SAUTÉ mode.

- Add garlic and fry for another minute.
- Add fish, coconut, and coconut milk and simmer on STEAM mod for 10 minutes.
- Place on a dish and serve it with boiled rice.

Glazed Salmon

(Time: 20 minutes \ Servings: 3)

INGREDIENTS

1 ½ cups of apricot nectar
2 tbsp. of honey
2 tbsp. of reduced sodium soy sauce
1 tbsp. of grated fresh ginger

2 minced cloves of garlic
¼ tsp. of cayenne pepper
¼ tsp. of ground cinnamon
¾ lb. of skinless salmon filet

DIRECTIONS

- Heat a 1 tbsp. of coconut oil in the Pressure cooker. Mix the apricot nectar, honey, soy sauce, ginger, garlic, cinnamon, and cayenne.
- Press the function Manual and set the timer to 10 minutes on STEAM mode. Close the lid and let the ingredients simmer.
- When the timer beeps, remove the ingredients, quick release the pressure, and remove around ¼ cup of the cooked glaze.
- Then remove the remaining glaze by putting it in a saucepan.
- Transfer the salmon into the Pressure cooker and brush it with some glaze; sauté it for 10 minutes. Serve with the remaining quantity of the glaze.

Teriyaki Salmon with Ginger

(Time: 10 minutes \ Servings: 3)

INGREDIENTS

¾ cup of Kikkoman Teriyaki
    Marinade
¾ cup of Teriyaki Marinade
2 tbsp. of brown sugar

1 tsp. of grated fresh ginger root
4 salmon steaks
1 tbsp. of coconut oil

DIRECTIONS

- In a large bowl, combine the Kikkoman Teriyaki, marinade, brown sugar, coconut oil, and grated ginger root.
- Heat 1 tbsp. of olive oil in the Pressure cooker and place the salmon. Pour the mixture over the salmon and press SAUTÉ.
- Cook for 10 minutes STEAM mode. Serve and enjoy this healthy piece of fish.

Desserts

Chocolate Pudding

(Time: 50 minutes \ Servings: 6)

INGREDIENTS:

1 cup milk
1 cup chocolate, melted
4 bananas, peeled, sliced
½ cup condensed milk

½ cup sugar
2 tablespoons butter
2 tablespoons cocoa powder
1 cup whipped cream

DIRECTIONS:

- In the Pressure cooker on SAUTÉ mode, add the butter and the whipped cream and cook until it is reduced to half.
- Add the condensed milk, chocolate, sugar, and cocoa powder and stir gradually.
- Pour half of the chocolate pudding into a large dish and place the banana slices evenly.
- Pour the remaining chocolate on top and freeze for 2 hours.

Lemon Cake

(Time: 50 minutes \ Servings: 6)

INGREDIENTS:

2 cups all-purpose flour
2 tablespoons lemon zest
2 tablespoons lemon juice
1 teaspoon baking powder
¼ teaspoon baking soda
½ cup butter

1 pinch salt
4 eggs
1 cup coconut milk
1 cup sugar
½ cup honey
½ cup apple jam

DIRECTIONS:

- In the Pressure cooker, place a stand or a trivet and add 2 cups of water.
- Combine the flour, sugar, salt, baking powder, baking soda, eggs, lemon juice butter, milk, and 1 tablespoon lemon zest and beat with electric beater.
- Transfer to a greased baking pan and place on a trivet, cover and cook on CAKE mode for 40 minutes.
- Combine the apple jam with honey. Pour this mixture onto the cake and top with lemon zest.

Chocolate Crackers

(Time: 40 minutes \ Servings: 6)

INGREDIENTS:

1 cup all-purpose flour
1 cup cocoa powder
½ cup molten chocolate
½ teaspoon baking powder

½ cup butter
2 eggs
1 cup caster sugar

DIRECTIONS:

- Grease the Pressure cooker with cooking spray. Combine all ingredients in a bowl and knead a soft dough.
- Roll out the dough on a clean surface. Cut with a cookie cutter.
- Place into the greased Pressure cooker and cook for 30 minutes on MANUAL mode.

Pumpkin and Pineapple Cobbler

(Time: 50 minutes \ Servings: 4)

INGREDIENTS:

1 cup ripe pumpkin, peeled, chunks
1 cup pineapple, chunks
1 cup milk

½ cup sugar
1 teaspoon pumpkin pie spice
1 cup whipped cream for toping

DIRECTIONS:

- In the Pressure cooker, add pumpkin, pineapples, milk, sugar, and pumpkin pie spice and cover.
- Cook on SLOW COOK mode for 50 minutes. Put on a serving dish and top with whipped cream.

Chocolate Silk Bowls

(Time: 35 minutes \ Servings: 4)

INGREDIENTS:

2 cups raw chocolate
¼ cup cocoa powder
2 tablespoons brown sugar

1 cup milk
¼ cup heavy cream
3 tablespoons butter

DIRECTIONS:

- Melt the butter in on SAUTÉ mode. Add milk, brown sugar, chocolate, and cream, and cook well on slow mode for 30 minutes.
- Stir occasionally. Place in small serving bowls and place inside the fridge for 10 minutes.

Pineapple and Mango Blossom

(Time: 50 minutes \ Servings: 3)

INGREDIENTS:

1 cup mango, chunks
1 cup pineapple slices
1 cup milk
½ cup sugar

½ teaspoons vanilla extract
1 cup whipped cream
½ cup pomegranates

DIRECTIONS:

- In the Pressure cooker, add milk, pineapple, sugar and mangoes cover with a lid.
- Cook for about 50 minutes on slow mode. Transfer to a serving dish when cooled.
- Add 2-3 spoons of whipped cream on top and sprinkle with pomegranates.

Mouth-melting Bread Pudding

(Time: 60 minutes \ Servings: 4)

INGREDIENTS:

6 slices of bread, roughly shredded
4 eggs
½ cup sugar
½ teaspoon cardamom powder
¼ teaspoon vanilla extract

1 cup milk
1 cup mozzarella cheese, shredded
1 pinch salt
1 tablespoon butter

DIRECTIONS:

- In a large bowl, beat eggs with a pinch of salt for 3-4 minutes.
- Transfer to the Pressure cooker, add the bread slices, milk, cardamom powder, butter, cheese, sugar, and vanilla extract.
- Cook for 60 minutes on SLOW COOK mode on low heat. Serve hot.

Pistachio Cake

(Time: 50 minutes \ Servings: 4)

INGREDIENTS:

2 tbsp. pistachio powder
4-5 tablespoons mint leaves, finely
   chopped
½ cup sugar
1 cup all-purpose flour

1 teaspoon vanilla extract
1 tablespoon cocoa powder
2 eggs
½ cup butter

DIRECTIONS:

- In a large bowl, beat the eggs until fluffy. In another bowl, beat the butter with sugar, add vanilla extract and beat for 1-2 minutes.

- Now add it to the eggs mixture and fold flour, vanilla extract, mint leaves, and pistachio powder.
- Pour the butter into the greased Pressure cooker and cover with a lid.
- Cook on CAKE mode for 45 minutes.

Banana and Strawberry Pudding

(Time: 40 minutes \ Servings: 3)

INGREDIENTS:

1 cup banana, slices
1 cub strawberries
2 cups milk

½ cup sugar
3 tablespoons honey
½ teaspoon cardamom powder

DIRECTIONS:

- In the Pressure cooker, add milk, banana, strawberries, sugar, and cardamom powder, cover with a lid.
- Cook for 40 minutes on SLOW COOK mode.
- Transfer to a dish and top with honey.

Buttercream Dessert

(Time: 24 minutes \ Servings: 2)

INGREDIENTS:

1 cup sugar
3 tbsp. almond flour
3 egg whites

4 tbsp. granulated sugar
2 tbsp. food color
4 cups buttercream for filling

DIRECTIONS:

- Add flour and sugar into a bowl. Mix egg whites, sugar and food color.
- Pour the batter into a round baking tray.
- Cook for 20 minutes in the pressure cooker on CAKE mode.
- When ready, pour the buttercream over it to serve!

Puff Pastry

(Time: 17 minutes \ Servings: 3)

INGREDIENTS:

2 cups Milk
1 tbsp. Vanilla bean extract
3 Egg yolks
2 tbsp. Sugar

2 tbsp. Cornstarch
3 tbsp. Butter
2 sheets Puff pastry
½ cup Confectioners' sugar

DIRECTIONS:

- Place puff pastry into a round baking tray. Add milk and vanilla bean extract into a bowl.
- Mix in the egg yolks, sugar, cornstarch and butter. Pour the mixture into the baking tray.
- Cook for 15 minutes in the pressure cooker on MANUAL mode. When ready, powder with confectioners' sugar to serve!

Chocolate Mix Recipe

(Time: 14 minutes \ Servings: 3)

INGREDIENTS:

½ cup heavy cream
2 tbsp. vanilla extract
2 cups flour
½ tbsp. salt

3 egg whites
1 cup sugar
2 cups chocolate chips
chocolate shavings to garnish

DIRECTIONS:

- Add flour and vanilla extract in a bowl. Mix in the salt, egg whites, chocolate and salt.
- Pour the mixture into a round baking tray. Cook for 10 minutes in the pressure cooker on MANUAL mode.
- When ready, cover the cake with heavy cream and chocolate shavings to serve!

Honey Pistachio Cake Recipe

(Time: 12 minutes \ Servings: 2)

INGREDIENTS:

2 cups butter
2 cups flour
2 tbsp. sugar
1 tbsp. brown sugar
¼ cup honey

3 egg whites
1 tbsp. baking powder
1 cup chopped pistachios
1 cup chopped almonds

DIRECTIONS:

- Add butter and flour in a bowl. Mix in the brown sugar, egg whites and baking powder.
- Pour the mixture into a round baking tray. Cook for 10 minutes in the pressure cooker on MANUAL mode.
- When ready, cover the cake with honey and garnish with pistachios. Add almonds to serve and enjoy!

Carrot and Honey Pie

(Time: 40 minutes \ Servings: 4)

INGREDIENTS:

1 cup shredded carrot
1 cup of milk
1 cup shredded mozzarella cheese
½ cup condense milk

1 teaspoon cardamom powder
4-5 almonds, chopped
4-5 pistachios, chopped
¼ cup sugar

DIRECTIONS:

- In the Pressure cooker, place carrots, milk, condense milk, mozzarella cheese, cardamom powder, and sugar and cover.
- Cook for 60 minutes on SLOW COOK mode.
- Transfer into a serving dish and top with chopped pistachios and almonds.

Cherry Delight

(Time: 40 minutes \ Servings: 3)

INGREDIENTS:

1 cup fresh cherries, chopped
½ cup pomegranates
2 cups milk
1 cup whipped cream

½ cup sugar
1 tsp. vanilla extract
1 pinch of salt
½ cup pineapple slices

DIRECTIONS:

- In the Pressure cooker, add cherries, milk, sugar, vanilla extract and salt, cover with a lid.
- Cook on MANUAL mode for 15 minutes. Serve with pomegranate, whipped cream and pineapples slices on top.

Conclusion

This book is an easy guide for you to follow if you wish to learn how to cook in pressure cooker. Mueller pressure cooker makes your life easier by giving you quick results. All the recipes can be cooked in mueller pressure cooker in no time, and you won't have to wait more than a few minutes. If you are getting to work late, then only 10 minutes for an mueller pressure cooker recipe will give you a delicious meal.

There are different kinds of recipes which you will be able to find in this book such as breakfast, lunch, side dishes, chicken and desserts. All the recipes are short and simple to understand. The ingredients are simple items which would be found in your kitchen. All you need is a great technique to have great food at any time of the day. Mueller pressure cooker gives you the means to cook any food in a short time. You do not have to deal with flames anymore because the electric pot will cook anything for you.

You can make a whole dinner with mueller pressure cooker. Once you know how to operate it and how to cook, then this efficient pot will give you excellent results. All the food recipes are cooked under hot air pressure which is generated by the mueller pressure cooker. The food is healthy and safe to eat. The variety of recipes found in this eBook will give you the ease to cook any recipe, whether it is breakfast, lunch, or dinner time. Check out the recipes and choose your favorite ones to cook in the mueller pressure cooker today!

Made in the USA
San Bernardino, CA
17 July 2018